SpringerBriefs in Finance

More information about this series at http://www.springer.com/series/10282

Victor U. Ekpu

Determinants of Bank Involvement with SMEs

A Survey of Demand-Side and Supply-Side Factors

 Springer

Victor U. Ekpu
Adam Smith Business School
   (Economics Division)
University of Glasgow
Glasgow
UK

ISSN 2193-1720   ISSN 2193-1739   (electronic)
SpringerBriefs in Finance
ISBN 978-3-319-25836-2   ISBN 978-3-319-25837-9   (eBook)
DOI 10.1007/978-3-319-25837-9

Library of Congress Control Number: 2015954578

JEL Classification Codes: G21, G28, G32, G34, L23

Springer Cham Heidelberg New York Dordrecht London
© The Author(s) 2016
This work is subject to copyright. All rights are reserved by the Publisher, whether the whole or part
of the material is concerned, specifically the rights of translation, reprinting, reuse of illustrations,
recitation, broadcasting, reproduction on microfilms or in any other physical way, and transmission
or information storage and retrieval, electronic adaptation, computer software, or by similar or dissimilar
methodology now known or hereafter developed.
The use of general descriptive names, registered names, trademarks, service marks, etc. in this
publication does not imply, even in the absence of a specific statement, that such names are exempt from
the relevant protective laws and regulations and therefore free for general use.
The publisher, the authors and the editors are safe to assume that the advice and information in this
book are believed to be true and accurate at the date of publication. Neither the publisher nor the
authors or the editors give a warranty, express or implied, with respect to the material contained herein or
for any errors or omissions that may have been made.

Springer International Publishing AG Switzerland is part of Springer Science+Business Media
(www.springer.com)

Preface

This monograph on the Determinants of Bank Involvement with SMEs is an excerpt from my doctoral study at the University of Glasgow (UK). It is a comprehensive yet concise reference text that brings together all facets of SME banking theories and empirical studies in one text. This study contains the latest policy debates on money creation and credit rationing and the relative role of demand-side and supply-side factors affecting SME financing. Readers will understand the borrower-specific, lender-specific and business environment drivers of (and obstacles to) bank finance for SMEs as well as the determinants of loan contract terms, particularly the risk premium and collateral. Readers will also understand how loan officers acquire proprietary information on SMEs and apply various lending techniques, such as financial statement lending, relationship lending and credit scoring to the loan underwriting process. This monograph also features recent trends on the rise of alternative finance intermediaries such as online peer-to-peer lenders and the competitive implications for traditional banks providing loans to SMEs.

Findings from this monograph will thus be of particular interest to commercial bankers, bank-dependent small-business borrowers as well as policy makers, and researchers in central banks, development banks, development agencies and international financial institutions. First, economic policy makers can understand from this study the factors affecting lenders' decisions to lend to SMEs including the factors that affect the quantity and cost of credit available to SMEs, which are crucial for improving SME lending policies. Second, banks may especially benefit from this study as it might help them to understand the profitability and economics of their lending methods, policies and business models and how to improve their SME risk management practices. Third, it is intended that the findings of this survey will also help improve the knowledge of bank-dependent SME borrowers with respect to understanding banks' requirements and expectations for loan applicants and users of loanable funds in order to better satisfy their banking and financial needs. The monograph can be used by academics as a textbook or supplementary material for business students taking banking and finance theory courses at undergraduate and postgraduate levels. It can also be used by institutions that offer professional courses in SME Banking. This book will also appeal to business consultants, investors, project financiers and business creditors.

Glasgow, UK   Victor U. Ekpu
August 2015

Contents

Part III Determinants of Credit Availability to SMEs

Abstract

This survey examines both theoretical and empirical literature on the demand- and supply-side factors affecting bank involvement with SMEs. It has been established that access to bank finance for SMEs is difficult and costly because they are relatively young and informationally opaque. SMEs tend to rely much on bank finance not just for their operational needs but also in order to build credit reputation early in their life cycle. The theoretical models upon which the foundation of bank lending is carried out are the money creation and credit rationing concepts. This survey reveals a number of debates on the relative role of money demand and supply in determining lending constraints, particularly the debate between the new Keynesians (mainstream economists) and the post-Keynesians (heterodox economists).

Broadly, the factors affecting credit availability to SMEs are categorized into two: demand-side and supply-side constraints. On the demand side, findings generally reveal that a borrower's size, credit reputation, availability and cost of proprietary information and bank size play a major role in a borrower's choice of financing source. A firm's characteristics, its owners' characteristics, bank–borrower relationships and demand-side market failures also determine the availability of credit to SMEs. On the supply side, bank organizational structure, risk appetite and cost factors, market structure, the type of lending technology adopted and the lending infrastructure are dominant factors. The determinants of risk premium on SME loans are largely connected with factors that underline the opacity and riskiness of SMEs such as firm size, firm age, firm credit rating, availability of collateral and quality of bank–borrower relationships. The determinants of the use and amount of collateral are largely associated with borrower and loan characteristics, particularly firm size, loan size and borrower's credit rating. External factors such as the business cycle, competition and other market structure factors also affect the extent to which collateral is used to secure credit transactions. The findings from this survey will be of interest to stakeholders in the SME lending market, particularly economic policy makers, commercial bankers and bank-dependent small-business borrowers.

Keywords Bank lending · SMEs · Demand side · Supply side · Credit rationing · Large banks · Small banks · Relationship lending · Credit scoring · Risk premium · Collateral

Part I
Introduction

Abstract Small and medium-sized enterprises (SMEs) are the backbone of most economies today, accounting for a large share of employment and business turnover. The availability of finance for SME borrowers has thus become an issue of crucial importance to most economies. This introductory part provides an overview of the demand and supply side factors that determine bank involvement with SMEs. It also explains the different financing options available to SMEs such as internally generated cash flows, personal finance (capital) from proprietors, debt finance (which includes bank finance), equity finance, and venture capital, highlighting the advantages and disadvantages of each financing source for the borrower. The final section shows evidence of bank finance as a very important component of external finance for SMEs, providing recent statistics of borrowers' dependence on various types of bank finance in US and UK.

Keywords SMEs · Economic importance · Financing options · Bank finance · Demand side · Supply side

Chapter 1
Bank Involvement with SMEs: Introduction

1.1 Background and Overview

The availability of bank finance to small and medium sized enterprises (SMEs) is an issue of topical debate among policy makers and practitioners around the world especially at this time of severe economic stress. SMEs are very crucial to the growth and success of most economies. SMEs account for between 60 and 70 % of jobs in most OECD countries, with a particularly large share in Italy and Japan and relatively smaller share in the US.[1] In the UK for instance, there are over 4.8 million SMEs, accounting for more than 50 % of employment and business turnover in UK.[2] SMEs also play a significant role in low and middle-income countries. For example, in Nigeria, SMEs account for about 70 % of industrial employment and 60 % of agricultural labour force (Lawal and Ijaiya 2007). Because small firms are innovative, flexible and adaptive, they have been described as vital and crucial to the strength of the economy as a whole. Sadly, however, due to their small scale of operations, most do not have adequate access to financial resources. In addition, the quality of service they receive from their banks and the terms on which those services are provided are key elements in determining the success of this sector. SMEs tend to face financing difficulties because they are relatively young, inexperienced and informationally opaque. Most of them also lack good credit reputation and are exposed to huge operational risks. Given these factors, when they eventually obtain credit from lenders, they do so at relatively high costs.

Since the onset of the global financial crisis in 2007, many banks around the world have reduced lending to small businesses due to the so-called "liquidity squeeze" and the claim by bank managers that they cannot find high quality applicants. While on the one hand, some commentators (e.g. media, government)

---

[1]See OECD publication: http://www.oecd.org/cfe/smes/2090740.pdf for more on the economic importance of SMEs.

[2]See HM Treasury (2010); see also Competition Commission, 2002, volumes 1–4 for details of a report on banking services to SMEs in UK.

© The Author(s) 2016
V.U. Ekpu, *Determinants of Bank Involvement with SMEs*,
SpringerBriefs in Finance, DOI 10.1007/978-3-319-25837-9_1

are of the opinion that banks (the supply side) are not adequately supporting viable businesses, bankers on the other hand, see the biggest driver of lending levels to be demand influenced by wider economic conditions and business confidence. Conventional wisdom teaches that the demand for bank loans naturally declines during a recession as businesses scale back on inventories and capital investment plans, while tending to build up cash reserves. Similarly, banks tend to tighten credit supply during financial crisis. Such a tightening in credit supply could be the result of a number of factors, including an increase in banks' cost of funds relative to the bank rate, or a reduction in risk appetite (Bell and Young 2010). However, in the light of the recent financial crisis, quantitative easing (the process by which a central bank injects more money directly into the economy) has helped to ameliorate the consequences of higher cost of funds, credit constraints and the risk of very low inflation (Bank of England 2009).

So the question remains, what is the relative influence between demand and supply in terms of the *availability* and *pricing* of loans? It is worth mentioning that for Post Keynesians, the availability of credit is demand determined but this is subject to an assessment of the borrower's creditworthiness, while neoclassicals believe that credit is supply determined. The post-Keynesian theory of endogenous money creation presupposes that money creation in a modern economy is ultimately dependent on the demand for credit, and not the supply of credit as most mainstream economists say (Pilkinton 2014). The Bank of England, in a recent paper (McLeay et al. 2014), finally endorsed the post-Keynesian endogenous money theory, though there are still a number of debates on the relative role of money demand and supply in determining lending constraints. The paper explains that the majority of money in the modern economy is created by commercial banks making loans, a phenomenon that is contrary to the money multiplier theory found in most macroeconomics textbooks—which is that banks simply act as intermediaries, lending out savings deposits that customers place with them.

Generally, the decision to grant the loan requests of small firms is a function of several factors. On the demand side, factors such as firm and owner characteristics, loan characteristics, availability of collateral, as well as firm-lender relationship characteristics play crucial roles in lending decisions. On the supply side, some of the major determinants of the willingness and ability of banks to extend credit to SME borrowers are the effects of bank size as well as other banking market characteristics. The micro-level factors determining loan contracts are connected largely to loan risk characteristics, firm and lender-specific characteristics, relationship characteristics, and external factors such as monetary policies, competition and the business cycle. There are also possible interdependencies between these set of variables. For example, the strength[3] of the borrower-lender relationships has been found to have significant effects on loan contract characteristics. Specifically,

---

[3]Berger and Udell (1995) used the length (duration) of borrower-lender relationship to measure the strength of relationship, while Petersen and Rajan (1994) utilised in addition to length other variables like the degree of a firm's use of non-loan related financial services as well as a measure of the firm's concentration of borrowing from a few lenders.

longer relationships were found to reduce loan rates and collateral requirements of banks (Petersen and Rajan 1994; Berger and Udell 1995). Bank characteristics have also been found to have effects on loan pricing and maturity (e.g. Hubbard et al. 2002; Coleman et al. 2002).

Research also shows that there are several factors that affect the use or non-use of the various lending technologies and therefore the extent to which banks lend to credit worthy transparent and opaque SMEs. Berger and Udell (2006) identify the financial institution structure and the lending infrastructure[4] as key elements in determining the availability and quantum of credit supplied by banks to SMEs using different lending technologies. Financial institution structure implies the market presence of different classes of financial intermediaries that provide credit, as well as the competition among these institutions. Berger and Udell (2006) identify three major categories, namely: large versus small banks; foreign owned[5] versus domestically owned and state-owned versus privately owned. A part of this review considers the dichotomy between large and small banks and excludes the latter two categories in order to keep the research focused on bank size features, which dominate the literature on SME lending. There is also considerable evidence that market concentration can affect the supply of credit to SMEs (Petersen and Rajan 1995). Other authors have raised concerns that the global consolidation of financial services namely through mergers and acquisitions can arguably have adverse effects—under certain market conditions—on the supply of credit to small businesses (e.g. Peek and Rosengren 1995; Levonian and Soller 1996; Berger and Udell 1996). This stems partly from the empirically negative association between bank size and allocation of assets to SME lending. Moreover, recent trends in deregulation and technological changes have also fuelled significant changes made in SME credit availability. On the one hand, deregulation has tended to favour large banks, with many of them expanding their scale and scope of operations both geographically and in product mix diversification with attendant effects on the future of SME lending. On the other hand, technological revolution, especially the use of small business credit scoring (SBCS) has fundamentally altered the nature of small business lending by large and small banks. While large banks are known to be able to make high-volume low-cost loans to customers over great distances using credit scoring, small banks have been reliant on relationship-based loans.

Next, this study examines the financing options available to SMEs and the rationale for bank finance for SMEs.

---

[4]The lending infrastructure refers to the rules and conditions provided mostly by governments or their regulatory agencies that affect financial institutions and their abilities to lend to different potential borrowers. According to Berger and Udell (2006), the lending infrastructure consists of three environments: (a) the information environment (b) The legal judicial and bankruptcy environment (c) the tax and legal environments.

[5]Foreign owned banks are typically part of a large banking group, and as such they have similar characteristics as large banks. They have a wholesale orientation and may therefore be disadvantaged in small business lending.

1.2 Financing Options for SMEs

SMEs generally follow a *pecking order* in their quest to raise external finance, i.e. they start with cheaper sources of funds and then graduate to costlier financing sources. Apart from internally generated cash flows such as retained earnings, capital from proprietors and financial support from families and friends for start-ups, small businesses find debt finance one of the relatively cheapest means of raising funds for their operations. Bank credit is an extremely convenient form of finance for the firm that has a good relationship with his banker (Bates and Hally 1982). Debt finance may be preferred to equity finance because it does not dilute share ownership. Moreover, it is less likely to transmit control over the business, except in instances where loan covenants and other contractual terms may cede a sizeable level of control to external creditors (Berger and Udell 2003). Debt finance may also reduce verification costs because outside creditors will have to bear the cost and time of monitoring the company's cash flows or project returns in the event that debt repayment is not forthcoming or is not paid in full. Optimal financial arrangements such as loan covenants and other debt contracts will help to reduce monitoring costs and exert corporate control over managers of the borrowing firm.

A borrower's choice of financing sources is likely to be a function of its 'credit history' and its 'investment opportunities' (Bhattarcharya and Thakor 1993: 7). According to Diamond (1991), new and inexperienced borrowers without a verifiable reputation prefer to borrow from banks, while older firms with well-established reputation choose the capital market. Rajan (1992), however, argues that when borrowers anticipate huge profitable project returns in the future, they prefer arm's length[6] (direct) financing. In other words, while Diamond's view that the borrower's reputation is a key factor in the choice of financing source is 'retrospective', Rajan's prediction is rather 'prospective' (Bhattarcharya and Thakor 1993: 38), i.e. dependent on future investment returns. In essence, it can be noted that the decision of a firm to choose to access funds from the capital market arises from the firm's financial growth life cycle. Many de novo firms use bank finance initially to gain credibility or build public image before accessing capital markets as they become more profitable.

Another interesting argument in the literature focuses on the conflict between debt and equity holders (see Campbell 1979). Here, small high-quality, innovative firms tend to prefer (bilateral[7]) bank finance to equity finance because they want to avoid the disclosure of private information to product market competitors or to third

---

[6]Arm's length debt here refers to financing sources which do not entail huge disclosure costs aside from publicly available information e.g. bondholders (See Rajan 1992).

[7]Bilateral financing is often characterised by a close relationship between a borrower and a lender and where because of this intimacy the lender does not require the borrower to disclose as much verifiable information to be able to access credit. Thus bilateral financing is less costly.

parties.[8] But Campbell's framework does not take into account the risk of conjecture on the part of interested third parties when they discover that a bank loan has been granted (see Yosha 1995). There can be scenarios particularly under multilateral[9] financing arrangements, where the private information of a borrowing firm could be disclosed by a bank to a product market competitor who has borrowed from the same bank. In fact, most models ignore the possibility of this kind of tensions between the issuers of securities, on the one hand and third parties on the other hand. This is especially the case with Diamond (1991) and Rajan (1992) where, since monitoring and control rights are of meagre importance to low risk firms, they may prefer (less informed) arm's length debt to (informed) bank finance.

It is possible for a borrower's financing choice to be adversely affected by information leakages. Firms whose probability of success cannot be ascertained when they invest in private knowledge-producing activities (i.e. R&D) might as well find multilateral financing more beneficial to bilateral financing since it is baseless to try to shield their proprietary information from the public. Conversely, if firms can significantly influence their chances of making profits, they may find that because of free riding by competitors, multilateral financing may not be a viable option (Bhattarcharya and Chiesa 1995; Yosha 1995).

Another potential source of finance for SMEs is venture capital (VC). It is hypothesised that the most inexperienced borrowers who lack managerial skills resort to this type of capital (e.g Chan et al. 1990), while those who can convince investors of their managerial skills but lack credit reputation tend to approach banks (e.g. Bhattarcharya and Thakor 1993). Larger firms who are both skilled in management and have a reputation for creditworthiness opt for capital market financing. It has been argued that small firms tend to be heavily reliant on bank finance as opposed to venture capital for a number of reasons: First, there are huge fixed costs associated with arranging venture capital finance and this may not be readily affordable by small firms (e.g. Cowling 1998). Most venture capital firms may not even be willing to admit small risky businesses and incur huge operational costs (e.g. Harrison and Mason 1986). There is also considerable evidence of the increasing unwillingness of small firms to dilute equity ownership to outsiders and thus risk losing their autonomy and control (e.g. Dow 1992).

---

[8]Interested third parties may be a regulator, the tax authority, or even the firm's own labour union (See Rice 1990).

[9]In contrast to bilateral financing, multilateral financing requires borrowers to disclose as much information as possible, and even to be audited to be able to convince lenders that they are credit worthy.

1.3   Rationale for Bank Finance for SMEs

SME borrowers are faced with a plethora of financing sources ranging from debt finance, equity capital and venture capital finance. However, there is considerable evidence to show that bank finance is more patronised and hence a very important component of SME finance. In a National survey of Small Business Finance (NSSBF) carried out by the US Federal Reserve Bank in 2003, it was found that 86.5 % of SMEs that required external finance obtained credit from commercial banks, which by far surpasses the share of other types of financial institutions (e.g. thrift institutions, credit unions, finance companies, etc) offering small business loans and other financial services (Mach and Wolken 2006). The survey classified small firms as those having net assets of $25 Million or less. Larger firms tend to gain access to public capital markets by issuing commercial papers and bonds, whereas smaller firms usually find it difficult to access these other sources of credit, and hence become bank-dependent.[10] According to the Annual Survey of Small Businesses in Scotland (2005), bank loans were the most often used source of finance (42 %), followed by bank overdraft (26 %). 11 % of small businesses obtained a grant, and a further 9 % used leasing or hire purchase arrangements, i.e. asset-based finance (pp. 153). In more recent results from the BERR's Annual Small Business Survey 2007/08, it was found that of the number of UK SMEs that sought external finance, 46 % resorted to bank loans, confirming the importance of Bank finance for small businesses (William and Cowling 2009: 09).

The rest of this study investigates in detail, the determinants of bank involvement with SMEs. Part 2 presents the theoretical framework, which considers the various theoretical views on money creation and credit rationing (Chap. 2) and a model of adverse selection under Asymmetric information (Chap. 3). In part 3, the study takes a closer look at the demand-side or borrower factors affecting bank lending to SMEs (Chap. 4) as well as the lender-specific and environmental factors constraining bank lending to SMEs (Chap. 5). Part 4 is dedicated to the determinants of loan contract terms, which specifically examine the determinants of risk premium on SME loans and the determinants of collateral (Chap. 6). The study concludes in Chap. 7.

References

Bank of England (2009) Quantitative easing explained: putting more money into our economy to boost spending. Bank of England. Available at http://www.bankofengland.co.uk/monetarypolicy/documents/pdf/qe-pamphlet.pdf. Accessed 23 Dec 2014

Bates J, Hally DS (1982) The financing of small business, 3rd edn. Sweet and Maxwell, London, 243 pp

Bell V, Young G (2010) Understanding the weakness of bank lending. Bank Engl Q Bull Q4:311–320

---

[10]In recent times, however, small firms have been able to access credit from the dotcoms.

Berger AN, Udell GF (1995) Relationship lending and lines of credit in small firm finance. J Bus 68:351–382

Berger AN, Udell GF (2006) A more complete conceptual framework for financing of small and medium enterprises. J Financ Bank 30(11):2945–2966

Berger AN, Udell GF (1996) Universal banking and the future of small business lending. In: Saunders A, Walter I (eds) Financial system design: the case for universal banking. Irwin Burr, Ridge, pp 559–627

Berger AN, Udell GF (2003) Small business and debt finance. In: Acs ZJ, Audretsch DB (eds) Handbook of entrepreneurship research. Kluver Academic Publishers, Great Britain, pp 299–328

Bhattacharya S, Chiesa G (1995) Proprietary information, financial intermediation, and research incentives. J Financ Intermed 4:328–357

Bhattacharya S, Thakor A (1993) Contemporary banking theory. J Financ Intermed 3:2–50

Campbell T (1979) Optimal investment financing decisions and the value of confidentiality. J Financ Quantit Anal 14:913–924

Chan Y, Siegel D, Thakor A (1990) Learning, corporate control and performance requirements in venture capital contracts. Int Econ Rev 31:365–381

Coleman DF, Esho N, Sharpe I (2002) Do bank characteristics influence loan contract terms? Australian Prudential Regulation Authority (APRA) Working Paper 2002-01

Cowling M (1998) Regional determinants of small firm loans under the U.K loan guarantee scheme. Small Bus Econ 11:155–167

Diamond DW (1991) Monitoring and reputation: the choice between bank loans and directly placed debt. J Polit Econ 99:689–721

Dow S (1992) The regional financial sector: a Scottish case study. Reg Stud 26(7)

HM Treasury (2010) Financing a private sector recovery. Department for Business Innovation and Skills (BIS). Available at https://www.gov.uk/government/uploads/system/uploads/attachment_data/file/253760/bis-10-1081-financing-private-sector-recovery.pdf. Accessed 08 June 2012

Harrison R, Mason C (1986) The regional impact of the small firms loan guarantee scheme in the United Kingdom. Reg Stud 20(6):535–550

Hubbard G, Kuttner K, Palia D (2002) Are there bank effects in borrowers' costs of funds? Evidence from a matched sample of borrowers and banks. J Bus 75(4):559–581

Lawal WA, Ijaiya MA (2007) Small and medium scale enterprises' access to commercial banks' credits and their contribution to GDP in Nigeria. Asian Econ Rev J Indian Inst Econ 49(3):360–368

Levonian ME, Soller J (1996) Small banks, small loans, small business. Weekly Letter, Federal Reserve Bank of San Francisco

Mach TL, Wolken JD (2006) Financial services used by small businesses: evidence from the 2003 Survey of Small Business Finance. Fed Reserve Bull A167–A195

McLeay M, Radia A, Thomas R (2014) Money creation in the modern economy. Bank Engl Q Bull Q1:1–14

Peek J, Rosengren S (1995) Small business credit availability: how important is the size of lender? Working Papers 95-5, Federal Reserve Bank of Boston

Petersen MA, Rajan RG (1994) The benefits of firm-creditor relationships: evidence from small business data. J Financ 49:3–37

Petersen MA, Rajan RG (1995) The effect of credit market competition on lending relationship. Quart J Econ 110:407–443

Pilkington P (2014) Bank of England endorses post-Keynesian endogenous money theory. Available at https://fixingtheeconomists.wordpress.com/2014/03/12/bank-of-england-endorses-post-keynesian-endogenous-money-theory/. Accessed 24 Dec 2014

Rajan RG (1992) Insiders and outsiders: the choice between informed and arm's-length debt. J Financ 47:1367–1400

Rice E (1990) Firms' reluctance to go public: the deterrent effect of financial disclosure requirements. mimeo, Harvard University

William M, Cowling M (2009) Annual small business survey 2007/08. Department for Business Enterprise and Regulatory Reform, Institute of Employment Studies

Yosha O (1995) Information disclosure costs and the choice of financing source. J Financ Intermed 4:3–20

Part II
Theoretical Framework

Abstract Lending activity is influenced by the foundational theories of money creation and credit rationing. This part invokes two contemporary debates between the post-Keynesians and the new Keynesians. The first debate is on the money creation theories, namely the loanable funds theory versus the endogenous money theory. The new Keynesians seem to support the loanable funds theory, which presupposes that banks simply act as intermediaries, lending out deposits that savers place with them to borrowers. On the other hand, the post-Keynesians assert that money is endogenously created, that is, new money (deposit) is created from loans made by banks. The amount of money created thus depends on the demand for credit. Loanable funds theory also suggests that lending is ultimately constrained by either the quantity or price of reserves, which is the interest rate. The post-Keynesians, however, disagree, arguing that banks simply respond to profitable opportunities and not the quantity or price of reserves. Accordingly, banks only lend when the risk-return profile is in their favour.

The second debate relates to the theory of credit rationing, that is, the information asymmetry versus asymmetric expectations theories. According to the new Keynesians view, either the borrower or lender does not have sufficient information about the risk and returns from an investment project. This presence of asymmetric information generates "adverse selection" and "moral hazard" effects, which explain why credit rationing may persist even in liberalised financial markets. Banks thus use interest rates as a screening device. On the other hand, the post-Keynesians argue that neither the lender nor the borrower knows the prospective yield of an investment project. There is therefore fundamental uncertainty about the risks and possible outcomes of the project. Fundamental uncertainty then leads to asymmetric expectations about the future probability of success of the project.

Keywords Money creation · Credit rationing · New Keynesians · Post-Keynesians · Loanable funds · Endogenous money · Asymmetric information · Asymmetric expectations

Chapter 2
Theoretical Views on Money Creation and Credit Rationing

2.1 Loanable Funds Theory Versus Post-Keynesian Endogenous Money Theory

In what appears to be an adequate explanation to how money is created in a modern fiat money system, the Bank of England recently published an article in its quarterly review published in March 2014 (i.e. McLeay et al. 2014). This paper literally rejects the conventional theories of bank lending and money creation (e.g. those found in macroeconomics textbooks like Krugman and Wells 2009; Mankiw 2011) and seems to endorse the endogenous money creation theory of Post-Keynesian heterodox economists. One major misconception in most macroeconomics textbooks alluded to by the Bank of England is that banks act simply as intermediaries, lending out the deposits that savers place with them. According to this view, deposits are typically 'created' by the saving decisions of households, and banks then 'lend out' those existing deposits to borrowers, for example to companies looking to finance investment or individuals wanting to purchase houses. In fact, when households choose to save more money in bank accounts, those deposits come simply at the expense of money that would have otherwise gone to companies in payment for goods and services. Saving does not by itself increase the deposits or 'funds available' for banks to lend (McLeay et al. 2014). Thus in essence, viewing banks as simply intermediaries ignores the fact that commercial banks are actually creators of deposit money. The Post-Keynesian Endogenous Money theory presupposes that as financial intermediaries, commercial banks have the capacity to create money. By lending money that they do not directly possess, commercial banks are in effect issuing money. For example, whenever a bank makes a loan, it simultaneously creates a matching deposit in the borrower's bank account, thereby creating new money. Though commercial banks create money through lending, their lending activities are however limited by prudential regulations, which imposes constraints as a way of maintaining the resilience of the financial system.

© The Author(s) 2016
V.U. Ekpu, *Determinants of Bank Involvement with SMEs*,
SpringerBriefs in Finance, DOI 10.1007/978-3-319-25837-9_2

Another area of misconception relates to the so-called "money multiplier approach" to the creation of money, which suggests that the central bank determines the quantity of loans and deposits in the economy by controlling the quantity of central bank money. According to this view, central banks implement monetary policy by choosing a quantity of reserves. And because, it is assumed that there is a constant ratio of broad money to base money, these reserves are then "multiplied up" to a much greater change in bank loans and deposits (McLeay et al. 2014). For this theory to hold, the amount of reserves must be a binding constraint on lending, and the central bank must directly determine the amount of reserves. According to the credit view of monetary policy, one channel through which changes in bank reserves (induced by open market operations) can affect real activity is by affecting the quantity of funds that banks have to lend (Bernanke and Lown 1991). This is mostly achieved by varying the reserve requirements of banks. Higher reserve ratios reduce the quantum of funds available for onward lending, and vice versa. Though the money multiplier approach is particularly useful in understanding how the amount of reserves is determined, it does not describe how money is created in the real world.

In practice nowadays, rather than controlling the quantity of reserves, central banks typically implement monetary policy by setting the price of reserves—that is, the interest rates. According to Coppola (2014), the perception that the quantity of reserves created drives the amount of loans granted by banks is wrong. This is because banks' decisions to lend are based on the availability of profitable lending opportunities at any given point in time. Lending is driven by the banks' risk appetite. Banks lend when the risk/return profile is in their favour. When it is not, no amount of extra reserve creation will make them lend. Monetary policy therefore focuses on the price of money, not its quantity, since changes in the price of money will influence the returns available to banks for lending and therefore their willingness to lend. The Bank of England's recent paper (McLeay et al. 2014) argues that the most important influence on money creation is the interest rate. It admits that monetary policy is the ultimate constraint on lending.

> The interest rate that commercial banks can obtain on money placed at the central bank influences the rate at which they are willing to lend on similar terms in sterling money markets — the markets in which the Bank and commercial banks lend to each other and other financial institutions... Changes in interbank interest rates then feed through to a wider range of interest rates in different markets and at different maturities, including the interest rates that banks charge borrowers for loans and offer savers for deposits. By influencing the price of credit in this way, monetary policy affects the creation of broad money". (McLeay et al. 2014: 8)

The transmission mechanism of monetary policy described by the Bank of England does relate perfectly with both the New-Keynesian literature and the Post-Keynesian endogenous money theory. But the Post-Keynesian literature, however, disagrees with the idea that the characterization of the setting of interest rates is the ultimate constraint to lending as the Bank of England posits (Pilkington 2014). For post-Keynesians, the amount of money created in the economy is ultimately dependent on the demand for credit. Though the supply price of credit (that is, the interest rate) will influence the demand for credit, the experiences of the global financial crises over the last few years do show that what truly drives credit creation and the supply of credit is of secondary importance (Pilkington 2014). Prior to the recent crises, most central banks operated a loose monetary policy: policy discount rates (including interest rates on large certificate of deposits CDs) were brought low, while other wholesale market funds and managed liabilities were exempted from prudential reserve requirements. In essence, banks were awash with liquidity so that evidence from the recent crises seems to refute the hypothesis that supply was constrained by shortage of loanable funds. Moreover, the lending boom that preceded the crisis was largely aided by the flow of cheap funds around the world, especially from Asian markets to the developed markets. However, from 2008, with the dramatic freezing of wholesale markets, this source of funding proved much less attractive. This has increased demand for other, more traditional funding sources, such as retail deposits, which in turn has increased the costs of banks raising funds for onward lending (BBA 2011).

2.2 Information Asymmetry and Credit Rationing

This sub-section presents two opposing views on the theory of credit rationing: the New Keynesian theory (or the mainstream view), pioneered by Stiglitz and Weiss (1981) and the post-Keynesian view. According to the current new-Keynesian mainstream economic theory, asymmetric information is widespread in financial markets. It generates "adverse selection" and "moral hazard" effects (as described in this section below), which explain why credit rationing may persist even in liberalised financial markets. For the post-Keynesian view, both adverse selection and moral hazard are unlikely to be serious problems in reality, so that the Stiglitz and Weiss model is unrealistic (Paloni 2014).

2.2.1 The New-Keynesian Theory—The Stiglitz and Weiss (S-W) Model

According to the New Keynesian theory of credit rationing, asymmetric information arises in credit markets between the borrower and lender when one of the counterparties (usually the lender) does not have sufficient information or knowledge of the other counterparty involved in the loan transaction, which makes it difficult to make accurate lending decisions. For example, a borrower who seeks a loan is believed to have better information about the potential returns and risk associated with the investment project for which the loan is sought than the lender does. In other words, the New Keynesian theory assumes that there is a precise probabilistic distribution of returns from each project that a potential bank borrower wants to undertake. This distribution is known by the borrower, but not by the lender. According to Stiglitz and Weiss (1981: 395), though the lender may know the expected mean return of a project, it cannot ascertain the riskiness of a project.

In market equilibrium, the presence of asymmetric information often leads to credit rationing among potential borrowers (Stiglitz and Weiss 1981; De Meza and Webb 1987; Berger and Udell 1992; Petersen and Rajan 1994). Banks making loans are concerned about the interest rate they receive on the loan and the riskiness of the loan. However, the interest rate a bank charges may itself affect the riskiness of the pool of loans in two ways, either by: (1) sorting potential borrowers ("adverse selection" effect); or (2) affecting the actions of borrowers ex-post (the incentive effect or "moral hazard"). Both effects derive directly from the residual imperfect information, which is present in loan markets after banks have evaluated loan applications (Stiglitz and Weiss 1981).

The adverse selection aspect of interest rates is a consequence of different borrowers having different probabilities of repaying their loan. The expected return to the bank depends on the probability of repayment, so the bank would like to be able to identify borrowers who are more likely to repay. It is difficult for the bank to identify "good borrowers", and to do so requires the bank to use a variety of screening devices. One of such screening devices is the *interest rate* that a borrower is willing to pay: those who are willing to pay high interest rates may, on the average, be worse risks; they are willing to borrow at high interest rates because they perceive their probability of repaying the loan to be low. As the interest rate rises, the average "riskiness" of those who borrow increases, possibly lowering the bank's profits. Similarly, as the interest rate and other terms of the contract change, the behavior of the borrower is likely to change ("moral hazard"). For instance, raising interest rates decreases the return on projects that succeed. Higher interest rates induce firms to undertake projects with lower probabilities of success but higher payoffs when successful.

2.2.2 The Post-Keynesian Theory of Credit Rationing

According to post-Keynesian theory, asymmetric information is in practice not very significant, suggesting that neither the lenders nor the borrowers know the prospective yield of an investment project. In their view, credit rationing exists because borrowers and lenders have asymmetric expectations about the probability of repayment (Paloni 2014). Thus, why the New Keynesians on the one hand believe that only one party (the lender) is uncertain about the riskiness of the borrower, the Post-Keynesians on the other hand believe that both the lender and borrower are oblivious of the probability of loan repayment. In other words, they believe that the there is *fundamental uncertainty* about the risks and possible outcomes of an investment project (Wolfson 1996). This uncertainty is believed to affect the criteria that banks use in forming judgments about the risk of repayment. Bankers, knowing that they do not know the future, only rely on assumptions and certain conventions in their credit assessment. They then form an opinion of the likelihood of repayment. For example, borrowers who have a history of repaying loans on time and continue to maintain a strong financial condition will be preferred. Bankers also take into cognisance the prevailing macroeconomic conditions in making their assessment of the riskiness of a potential loan. Post-Keynesians thus argue that with fundamental uncertainty, the past provides no dependable guide to future events. They argue that investment is subject to uncertainty and not risk (Paloni 2014). For example, the outcome of an investment project depends upon future economic circumstances, future inventions, as well as the actions of future competitors. The argument is that even if similar investments have been made in the past, the economic environment of a new investment differs from those of past investments. This is the probability theory upon which the post-Keynesians assume information asymmetry cannot be used in these circumstances because uncertain outcomes are not constrained to any known finite set of possibilities (Paloni 2014).

Following from the concept of fundamental uncertainty, post-Keynesians also introduce the concept of *asymmetric expectations*, which suggests that both the lender and borrower will evaluate the future differently (i.e. they will reach different conclusions about the future) since they are both uncertain about the future, thus showing that they have asymmetric expectations about the future probability of any particular project (Wolfson 1996). Since the borrower and lender do not necessarily agree on the riskiness of a particular project, credit rationing tends to occur based on this uncertainty. One implication of this is that the lender will be more risk-averse than the borrower. In line with a Post Keynesian perspective of credit rationing, Wolfson (1996) argues that bankers accommodate all credit-worthy demands for credit, and ration all those demands not deemed creditworthy. According to him, a perceived change in the financial condition of bank borrowers will be likely to change bankers' conventional valuations of the risk of lending, and thus the extent of credit rationing. As Minsky (1986) argues, this change in valuation takes place endogenously. According to him, financial fragility increases as borrowers take on more debt, as the maturity of that debt shortens, and as liquidity declines. These borrower risk characteristics are examined in detail within the context of SME lending in Sect. 4.1.

References

Berger AN, Udell GF (1992) Some evidence on the empirical significance of credit rationing. J Polit Econ 100(5):1047–1077

Bernanke BS, Lown CS (1991) The Credit Crunch. Brookings Pap Econ Act 2:205–247

British Bankers Association (2011) Small Business lending bank facts, published 10/08/2011. http://www.bba.org.uk/media/article/small-business-lending-bankfacts/press-pack/. Accessed 20 Apr 2013

Coppola F (2014) The money multiplier is dead. Pieria, 13 Mar 2014. Available at: http://www.pieria.co.uk/articles/the_money_multiplier_is_dead. Accessed 30 Dec 2014

De Meza D, Webb DC (1987) Too much investment: a problem of asymmetric information. Quart J Econ 102:281–292

Krugman P, Wells R (2009) Macroeconomics, 2nd edn. Macmillan Higher Education, New York, 524p

Mankiw NG (2011) Principles of macroeconomics, 6th edn. Cengage Learning, Boston, 576p

McLeay M, Radia A, Thomas R (2014) Money creation in the modern economy. Bank Engl Q Bull Q1 1–14

Minsky H (1986) Stabilizing an unstable economy. Yale University Press, New Haven

Paloni A (2014) Banking sector development, rationing and the funding of innovation. In: Lecture notes on Financial Institutions and Markets in Developing Countries, Adam Smith Business School, University of Glasgow

Petersen MA, Rajan RG (1994) The benefits of firm-creditor relationships: evidence from small business data. J Finance 49:3–37

Pilkington P (2014) Bank of England endorses post-Keynesian endogenous money theory. Available at: https://fixingtheeconomists.wordpress.com/2014/03/12/bank-of-england-endorses-post-keynesian-endogenous-money-theory/. Accessed 24 Dec 2014

Stiglitz J, Weiss A (1981) Credit rationing in markets with imperfect information. Am Econ Rev 71:393–410

Wolfson MH (1996) A post Keynesian theory of credit rationing. J Post Keynesian Econ 18 (3):443–470

Chapter 3
A Simplified Model of Adverse Selection in Loan Markets

According to the new Keynesian doctrine, the presence of asymmetric information in loan markets often leads to "adverse selection" and "moral hazard", resulting in credit rationing among potential borrowers (these concepts have been examined in Chap. 2). This chapter provides a simplified version of Stiglitz and Weiss's (1981) influential model of adverse selection and loan contracts determination. First, let's make some initial assumptions about the economic agents involved in a loan contract.

1. There are two types of borrowers: "good borrowers" and "bad borrowers". A proportion, q, of all borrowers is of the good type. They invest £1 and after one year get $1 + R_0$ (the expected return on a good project). A proportion, $1 - q$ of all borrowers is of the bad type. They invest £1 and after one year get $1 + R_1$ with probability of P of success and 0 with probability $1 - P$ of no success.
2. The firm profits are an increasing function of the riskiness of the project and hence the return on the project.
3. The return on a good project is greater than the expected return on a bad project with probability of success P, so that $1 + R_0 > P(1 + R_1)$. However, if a bad firm succeeds, it makes more money than a good firm (because high risks attract high returns) so that the realized earnings from a risky (bad) venture is always greater than the return from a good project: $1 + R_0 < 1 + R_1$.
4. The interest rate, i, is a screening device for distinguishing between good and bad credit risks.
5. The credit market considered here is assumed to be competitive. If the credit market is perfectly competitive, the profit to the bank from lending £1 will equal the cost of borrowing £1 from the public (so that interest rate, i, charged to borrowers equals the deposit rate, r). Banks can get funds by paying a deposit rate of r, where $r < R_0 < R_1$.
6. The expected return on a loan to a bank is decreasing function of the interest rate. The argument here is that adverse selection of interest rates could cause the returns to the bank to decrease with increasing interest rates hinged on the premise that as the interest rate increased, the pool of applicants became worse.

© The Author(s) 2016
V.U. Ekpu, *Determinants of Bank Involvement with SMEs*,
SpringerBriefs in Finance, DOI 10.1007/978-3-319-25837-9_3

3.1   Solution of the Model Under Perfect Information

In a world with perfect and costless information, the bank is able to distinguish between good and bad borrowers. Thus, it will specify precisely all the actions that the borrower could undertake (which might affect the return to the loan). However, the bank is not able to directly control all the actions of the borrower; therefore it will formulate the terms of the loan contracts in a manner designed to induce the borrower to take actions, which are in the interest of the bank, as well as to attract low-risk borrowers.

On the assumption of perfect information, banks charge two different interest rates: i_g and i_b for the good and bad borrowers, respectively:

$$1 + i_g = 1 + r \quad \text{No profit condition} \tag{3.1}$$

i.e. the revenue from lending to good firms = cost of borrowing from the public (hence profit = 0)

$$(1 + i_b)P = 1 + r \quad \text{Condition for bad borrowers} \tag{3.2}$$

i.e. banks will only lend to bad firms with probability P (that the success of the project is certain).

3.1.1   Intuitions

From Eq. (3.1), $i_g = r$, and this implies that the interest from good borrowers are paying off depositors, so that they are certain to borrow at this rate. More so, good borrowers will accept the rate because $i_g = r < R_0$—the interest they will pay is less than the return on the project.

Equation (3.2) implies that

$$i_b = \frac{(1+r)}{P} - 1 > r \quad (\text{since } P < 1) \tag{3.3}$$

This means that the interest rate charged on bad borrowers is greater than r (because of the riskiness of their project). Bad borrowers will borrow if $i_b < R_1$.

Bad borrowers will be excluded only if it is socially efficient to do so:

$$\text{If } P \text{ is small enough, } i_b > R_1 \quad \text{Bad borrowers are excluded} \tag{3.4}$$

$$\text{If } P \text{ is large enough, } i_b < R_1 \quad \text{Bad borrowers are participants} \tag{3.5}$$

From Eq. (3.4), bad borrowers are excluded if $i_b > R_1$, i.e. if $\frac{(1+r)}{P} - 1 > R_1$.

Rearranging:

$$\frac{(1+r)}{P} > 1 + R_1 ==> 1 + r > P(1 + R_1)\tag{3.6}$$

where $P(1 + R_1)$ is the expected return on a "bad" project.

To be in the interest of society, i.e. to be socially efficient, a project must have a return that at least compensates the providers of fund, i.e. depositors.

3.2 Solution of the Model Under Asymmetric Information

Under imperfect information condition, borrowers are assigned randomly to banks. Banks are able to tell the proportion of good borrowers (q) and the proportion of bad borrowers ($1 - q$), but they cannot distinguish between them in a pool of loan applicants in the market. Thus, by the law of large numbers, each bank finances a pool of random borrowers with expected return $(1 + i)$ for good firms and $P(1 + i)$ for bad firms.

It is important to note here that banks can only charge one interest rate since they lack complete on the credit worthiness of borrowers:

$$q = (1 + i) + (1 - q)P(1 + i) = 1 + r\tag{3.7}$$

From Eq. (3.7),

$$i = \frac{1 + r}{q + (1 - q)P} - 1\tag{3.8}$$

Notice: that if $q = 1$, then $i = r$ (this means that if all borrowers are good, then they will be charged at the deposit rate).

If $P = 1$, then $i = r$ (this means that if the probability of success of all projects is 1 then interest charged = deposit rate).

However, if $q < 1$ and $P < 1$, then $i > r$.

Note three (3) possibilities:

1. If $r < i < R_0 < R_1 \rightarrow$ Both good and bad borrowers participate in the market since the interest rate they are charged (i) is less than returns from both types of project
2. If $r < R_0 < i < R_1 \rightarrow$ Good borrowers are excluded from the market since the return is less than the interest rate charged. Here all socially efficient projects are not carried out because $i > R_0$.
3. If $r < R_0 < R_1 < i \rightarrow$ Both good and bad borrowers are excluded from the market since the return is less than the interest rate charged).

Intuition: Under asymmetric information, the credit market might malfunction in the sense that good borrowers can be excluded from it. Excluding good borrowers from the market is always socially inefficient.

3.3   Tools to Help Solve Adverse Selection Problems

According to Mishkin (2010), a number of options are available to banks to help solve the problems posed by adverse selection:

Screening of Investment Projects: Banks can collect detailed information regarding the feasibility of the borrowing firm's proposed project in order to determine the potential risks and returns of the project, and hence ascertain the worthwhileness of the project. In a pool of loan applicants, banks select the project (s) with the most promising returns and the lowest possible risk of failure or loss.

Past Credit Records: Banks can also screen loan applicants by assessing their previous credit history in order to determine their creditworthiness or ability to repay a loan. If a firm has previously borrowed from a bank or other banks, the lending bank can take a look at the borrowers' history of loan repayments. The lender can also look at the borrower's financial statement or checking account to examine its cash flow pattern and the firm's financial dealings with its customers, suppliers, or other economic agents doing business with it. Petersen and Rajan (1994) also suggest an alternative way to observing a borrower's credit reputation: by looking at how late the borrower pays its trade credit.

Private Production and Sale of Information: Banks can also rely on the privately produced information of other banks or credit rating agencies that may have conducted similar credit assessments on the firms they wish to lend to. Such privately produced information may help distinguish between good and bad firms. In the US, companies such as Standard and Poor's and Moody's gather information on firms' balance sheet positions and investment activities, publish these data, and sell them to subscribers—individuals, libraries, and financial intermediaries involves in purchasing securities or lending to firms.

The Use of Collateral: Adverse selection interferes with the functioning of credit market only if a lender suffers a loss when a borrower is unable to make loan payments and thereby defaults. Collateral, which is property promised to the lender if the borrower defaults, reduces the lender's losses in the event of a default. If a borrower defaults on a loan, the lender can sell the collateral and use the proceeds to make up for the losses on the loan. Lenders are thus more willing to make loans secured by collateral, and borrowers are willing to supply collateral because the reduced risk for the lender makes it more likely they will get the loan in the first place and perhaps at a better loan rate. The determinants of collateral are examined later in Sect. 6.2.

Assessing the Borrower's Net worth or Equity Capital: Net worth, the difference between a firm's assets (what it owns) and its liabilities (what it owes), can perform a similar role to collateral. If a firm has a high net worth, then even if it engages in investments that cause it to have negative profits and so defaults on its debt payments, the lender can take title to the firm's net worth, sell it off, and use the proceeds to recoup some of the losses from the loan. In addition, the more net worth a firm has in the first place, the less likely it is to default, because the firm has a cushion of assets that it can use to pay off its loans. Hence, when firms seeking credit have high net worth, the consequences of adverse selection are less important and lenders are more willing to make loans.

Building Long Term Relationships: Banks are able to monitor the credit risks of firms when they build long-standing relationships with them. The longer the duration a bank deals with a firm, the less likely that the firm will default on its debts, for fear of breaching the relationship and thereby losing access to funds in the future. Moreover, banks can obtain information about borrowers who have had long-term dealings with them by observing their credit history. For example, if a prospective borrower has had a checking or savings account or other loans with a bank over a long period of time, the loan officer can take a look at past activity on the accounts and learn quickly about the borrower (Nakamura 1994; Boot 2000). Thus, long-term customer relationships reduce the costs of information collection and make it easier to screen out bad credit risks. A detailed analysis on relationship lending techniques is examined in Sect. 5.3.1.

3.4 Tools to Help Solve Moral Hazard Problems

As noted earlier, banks would like borrowers to behave in a "good" way, that is, in a way that assures a predictable income to the firm. Firms on the other hand may want to behave in a more risky way that would allow them to earn large profits if they succeed but would leave them bankrupt otherwise. This is known as "moral hazard". This is the risk that the borrower will engage in activities that are undesirable from the lenders' point of view because they make it less likely that the loan will be paid back. Again, according to Boot et al. (1991), Berger and Udell (2003) and Mishkin (2010), banks have a number of options to mitigate moral hazard problems:

Collateral: When borrowers have more at stake because the collateral they have pledged to the lender is valuable, the risk of moral hazard—the incentive to act in a manner that lenders find objectionable—will be greatly reduced because the borrowers themselves have a lot to lose. Another way of describing the solution that collateral provides to the moral hazard problem is to say that it makes the debt contract *incentive-compatible*, that is, it aligns the incentives of the borrower with those of the lender (Mishkin 2010). The greater the borrower's collateral pledged, then the greater the borrower's incentive to behave in the way that the lender expects and desires, the smaller the moral hazard problem in the debt contract, and the easier it is for the firm to borrow. Conversely, when the borrower's collateral is lower, the moral hazard problem is greater, and it is harder to borrow.

Personal Guarantees: Personal guarantees are another important contracting tool in SME lending. According to Berger and Udell (2003), when entrepreneurs personally guarantee loans to their businesses, they convey contingent claims on their personal assets to the lender. This claim gives the lender legal recourse against the entrepreneur (or other guarantor) for any deficiency in the loan's repayment. In other words, if the business cannot fully repay its loan, the bank has recourse for any shortfall against the entrepreneur. Personal guarantees operate in a similar manner to outside collateral with three important distinctions. First, recourse under outside collateral is limited to the specific personal assets pledged as collateral, while a personal guarantee generally conveys a claim against the entire wealth of the guarantor. Second, outside collateral conveys a significant measure of control over the specific assets pledged to the lender. In particular, the collateral cannot be sold without the permission of the lender (the lienholder). However, in the case of a personal guarantee, no control over any personal assets is conveyed to the lender. Thus, the lender has no assurance that the entrepreneur (i.e. the guarantor) will have any remaining assets if the firm fails to repay a loan in the future. Third, legislation may limit a general claim operating through a guarantee against the entrepreneur's personal assets. For example, some countries may have laws that protect personal residences against general creditors in bankruptcy (Berkowitz and White 2004; Berger et al. 2011).

Monitoring and Enforcement of Restrictive Covenants: Restrictive covenants are directed at reducing moral hazard either by ruling out undesirable behavior or by encouraging desirable behavior. There are four (4) types of restrictive covenants that achieve this objective: (a) *Covenants to discourage undesirable behavior*: e.g. restrictions to undertaking risky investment projects, or covenants that mandate that a loan can be used only to finance specific activities, such as purchase of particular equipment or inventories; (b) *Covenants to encourage desirable behavior*: e.g. covenants that specify that the firm maintains minimum holdings of certain assets relative to the firm's size. This is to keep the borrower's net worth high because higher borrower net worth reduces the risk of moral hazard and makes the lender less likely to suffer losses; (c) *Covenants to keep collateral valuable*: Because collateral is an important protection for the lender, restrictive covenants can encourage the borrower to keep collateral in good condition and make sure that it stays in the possession of the borrower. For example, if a house is used as collateral, a restrictive covenant may require the house to be adequately insured in order to keep the collateral valuable; (d) *Covenants to provide information*: Restrictive covenants may also require a borrowing firm to provide information about its activities periodically in the form of quarterly accounting and income reports, thereby making it easier for the lender to monitor the firm and reduce moral hazard. This type of covenant may also stipulate that the lender has the right to audit and inspect the firm's books at any time.

3.5   Credit Rationing and the Use of Loan Commitments

Banks have also reduced the incidence of credit rationing by making loan commitments to their business borrowers. A loan commitment is a promise to lend in the future at the borrower's discretion on terms that are pre-specified. A great deal of commercial bank lending is done under commitments. One of the reasons for engaging in loan commitments is that it helps to reduce rationing (Bhattacharya and Thakor 1993). A loan commitment enables a bank to both guarantee credit availability and to process credit risk. Secondly, because loan commitments come at a fee which is paid upfront by the borrower, they help to ameliorate "moral hazard" at the time the borrower makes an investment decision. A third reason for being interested in loan commitments is that they enable banks to more efficiently manage their financial and reputational capital (see Bhattacharya and Thakor 1993). The sale of loan commitments can also facilitate the bank's planning by helping it to estimate future loan demand. A fourth reason is that loan commitments can frustrate monetary policy. An increase in short term interest rates, created by monetary policy initiative to reduce bank lending, will lead to greater takedowns under commitments as pre-committed borrowing rates look more attractive relative to spot rates.

References

Berger AN, Udell GF (2003) Small business and debt finance, book chapter. In: Acs ZJ, Audretsch DB (eds) Handbook of entrepreneurship research. Kluwer Academic Publishers, Great Britain, pp 299–328

Berger AN, Frame WS, Ioannidou V (2011) Reexamining the empirical relation between loan risk and collateral: the roles of collateral characteristics and types. Federal Reserve Bank of Atlanta Working Paper Series, Sept 2011–2012

Berkowitz J, White MJ (2004) Bankruptcy and small firms' access to credit. RAND J Econ 35 (1):69–84

Bhattacharya S, Thakor A (1993) Contemporary banking theory. J Financ Intermediation 3:2–50

Boot AWA (2000) Relationship banking: what do we know? J Financ Intermediation 9:7–25

Boot AWA, Thakor AV, Udell GF (1991) Secured lending and default risk: equilibrium analysis, policy implications and empirical results. Econ J 101:458–472

Mishkin FS (2010) The economics of money, banking and financial markets, 9th edn. Pearson, 664 pp

Nakamura LI (1994) Small borrowers and the survival of the small bank: is mouse bank mighty or Mickey? Federal Reserve Bank of Philadelphia Business Review (Nov/Dec), pp 3–15

Petersen MA, Rajan RG (1994) The benefits of firm-creditor relationships: evidence from small business data. J Financ 49:3–37

Stiglitz J, Weiss A (1981) Credit rationing in markets with imperfect information. Am Econ Rev 71:393–410

Part III
Determinants of Credit Availability to SMEs

Abstract The availability of credit to SMEs is influenced by a number of demand-side and supply-side factors, which could manifest under firm-specific, bank-specific and external or environmental factors. Findings from the demand side generally reveal that banks, especially large ones, tend to be attracted to larger, older, well-established and more financially secure firms. Relationship-driven banks tend to pay more attention to applicants that have pre-existing loan and deposit relationships with them. Banks are also more likely to demand collateral from young and inexperienced SME borrowers. This is because SMEs are known to be risky and have high failure rate. Whilst smaller banks have longer and more exclusive personal relationships with SME borrowers, large multi-office banks tend to have more short-lived, less exclusive and distant relationships with their customers. Findings from the supply side show that banks that have a relatively flatter organisational structure (such as smaller banks) tend to have advantages in loan monitoring and increased loan officer discretion. However, large banks with multi-office structures find it extremely costly to invest in relationships. Banks that are largely geared towards SMEs are known to be heavily reliant on relationship lending techniques, whilst large multi-office banks tend to have advantages in economies of scale and scope because they rely on transactions-based lending and other financial management services. Regulatory factors such as enforcement of capital requirements, sectoral credit limits and monetary policies also affect the quantity and cost of loanable funds via lenders' risk appetite, credit rationing and the credit channel, respectively. Banking consolidation also tends to affect the amount of SME lending as lending generally reduces after a merger or acquisition. The type of lending technology adopted and the lending infrastructure are also dominant factors affecting the supply of credit to SMEs.

Keywords Credit availability · SMEs · Demand side · Supply side · Large banks · Small banks

Chapter 4
Demand-Side Factors Affecting Bank Lending to SMEs

A number of demand-side factors affect the supply of bank loans, including: *firm* and *owner* characteristics, *borrower-lender relationship* characteristics as well as *demand-side market failures*. This chapter now reviews all of them in detail.

4.1 Firm Characteristics

Generally, lenders are willing to extend credit only when they have high expectations that the borrower is able to repay. The less a banker knows about a firm, the more information the firm must provide to be able to make a convincing case for receiving a loan (Barrett 1990). Thus, banks are likely to favour borrowers that exhibit characteristics that assure the bank of the chance of being repaid. Sadly, however, most small businesses suffer disproportionately from adverse selection because they are both more reliant on external finance and relatively more opaque than older and larger firms.

4.1.1 Firm Size

A firm's size is usually measured in different ways, most notably, asset size, annual sales or turnover. It is expected that a larger firm will be more credit worthy because it is well established and typically more diversified than a smaller firm so that it is more likely to be approved for a loan (Cole et al. 2004; Cole 2008). On the other hand, it is generally believed that smaller firms are more prone to insolvency than large firms because they are usually less diversified on the production and distributions side and are more likely to face financing constraints (Behr and Guttler 2007). This notion is taken into consideration by banks that do not grant credit to high-risk borrowers.

© The Author(s) 2016
V.U. Ekpu, *Determinants of Bank Involvement with SMEs*,
SpringerBriefs in Finance, DOI 10.1007/978-3-319-25837-9_4

4.1.2   Firm's Age/Transparency

A borrowing firm's age could affect the inclination of lenders to extend credit to it. Older firms are thought to be more credit worthy because they have an established track record and are relatively stable and less risky. They are also less opaque and relatively easy for a lender to scrutinise and monitor. Empirical evidence shows that large banks tend to be attracted to older, more established and financially stable firms (Haynes et al. 1999). Transparency on the other hand, has to do with the availability of financial records and/or audited financial statements. It is expected that a firm that has good financial records will be able to convince a bank of its ability to repay a loan. Incidentally, most young SMEs suffer financial constraints because they are more informationally opaque than older and large firms. A business is said to be opaque if outsiders (e.g. creditors, competitors, investors or rating agencies) cannot easily determine its quality or ascertain its credit worthiness and hence its likelihood to repay a loan given these information asymmetries (Hyytinen and Parajarinen 2008).

Banks, especially large ones, rely hugely on audited financial statements as an important piece of information in commercial lending decisions. Since large banks rely more on hard information than do small (relationship) banks, they are more likely to approve loans for firms with better financial records (mostly in the form of audited financial statements), and these have often been proved to be relatively older and more transparent firms (Haynes et al. 1999; Kim 2008). In other words, large banking institutions tend to lend to relatively transparent and safer borrowers that are likely to earn transactions credits. On their part, small business borrowers may find it prohibitively expensive to engage the services of auditors and hence are attracted to smaller (relationship) banks that rely mostly on non-financial information in order to accommodate the opacity of the small business borrower.

4.1.3   Firm Profitability/Financial Performance

The past financial performance or profitability of a firm is an important indicator of its ability and capacity to repay a loan (e.g. Berry et al. 1993). Profitability is usually measured by the firm's *return on assets (ROA)* or *return on equity (ROE)*, among other measures. Lenders generally expect that a firm with greater profitability will be able to demonstrate ability to service its debts out of its earnings. According to Bruns and Fletcher (2008: 13), "past profitability shows the firm's past operational success and thus provides tangible representations of the competence of the SME". A company is able to demonstrate its ability to repay a loan through the strength of its financial statements. According to Berger and Udell (2003, 2006), there are two important ingredients to the use of financial statement lending technology. First, the borrower must have informative financial statements (e.g. audited statements prepared by reputable accounting firms according to widely accepted accounting standards such as GAAP or IFRS). Second, the borrower must have a strong financial condition as reflected in the financial ratios calculated from these statements.

The main purpose of accounting information is for lenders and other potential investors to make rational financing decisions (Kam 1990). Financial ratios calculated from financial statements (e.g. cash flow, profit/loss and balance sheet statements) have been found to be reliable predictors of corporate bankruptcy by some notable researchers (e.g. Beaver 1967; Altman 1968, 1993; Ohlson 1980), which indicate their importance in the prediction of credit defaults. Therefore, information on past financial performance (obtained from financial ratios) allows banks to assess the creditworthiness of a particular firm. Although a loan contract may have different contracting elements, including collateral, personal guarantees and/or loan covenants, the lender will view the expected future cash flow of the company as the primary source of repayment. Any unanticipated defaults will then be compensated for by other mitigants such as collateral and guarantees.

4.1.4 Financial Stability (Leverage and Liquidity)

A major concern in SME lending is the lack of an adequate equity stake or enough retention of earnings to boost equity (Hutchinson and McKillop 1992). Two main determinants of financial stability for businesses are *leverage* or *gearing* and *liquidity* or *cash flow*. There are two measures commonly used in the empirical literature for measuring leverage: the *ratio of debts to assets* or the ratio of *debt to equity* (see Berry et al. 1993; Cole et al. 2004). Bankers often use the latter where the owners' equity stake or retained earnings is considered important. Berry et al. (1993) however, show that the calculation of the gearing level of businesses is not straightforward as the basis of usage is not common among all banks or bankers. In some cases, gearing is referred to the business as a whole, while in other cases a banker might consider the gearing of the particular lending proposition. There have also been cases that showed that what may have been an acceptable level of gearing to a banker when the lending was within that banker's mandate was less acceptable if the request had to be referred to a more senior level (see, for example, Dewhurst and Burns 1989: 104). However, according to Berry et al. (1993), four factors seem to influence the acceptable norms with respect to leverage (1) the size of business and the stage of its development, (2) the purpose of the borrowing (e.g. working capital or project finance), (3) the type of finance required (whether short term or long term), and (4) the type of business. The bottom line here is that highly leveraged firms are riskier and have greater chances of defaulting on a bank loan because huge levels of indebtedness affects their ability to service their debts or even retain earnings. Cole et al. (2004) found that these firms are however more likely to apply to larger banks who can hold riskier, yet more profitable asset portfolios.

The second measure of financial stability is the *firm's liquidity*. This is usually measured by the ratio of a firm's *cash assets to total assets*. Firms with more liquid assets are generally thought of as being credit worthy since they can convince lenders of their ability to meet their current financial obligations (Cole 2008). A banker can assess the borrower's liquidity level by monitoring the flow of funds in and out its bank accounts (Berry et al. 1993; Nakamura 1994). This sort of monitoring tells a great deal how the business managers are managing its working capital. It also "provides the early warning system for potential problems" and is also used to form judgments on the ability of the SME owner to run the business profitably (Berry et al. 1993: 146). On the link between a firm's liquidity and the type of lender, Cole et al. (2004) finds that firms with more liquid assets tend to apply to larger banks. This is perhaps due to the fact that they are able to obtain larger loan amounts from large banks.

4.1.5   Firm's Organisational Form

A firm's organisational form (i.e. whether it's a *sole proprietorship, partnership, limited company or limited partnership*) might matter in the lending decisions of banks. The degree of informational asymmetry and the magnitude of agency conflicts between owners, managers and creditors are likely to vary with organizational form (Cole 1998). Moreover the nature of a firm's liabilities is also likely to be a function of its organizational form. Typically, proprietorships or non-corporate institutions are assumed to be more credit worthy than partnerships and corporations, *ceteris paribus*, because a lender can liquidate or sell both the personal assets and business assets of the owner to fulfill a claim (Berkowitz and White 2004). In the same vein, a lender might prefer to lend to a partnership other than a corporation as it can lay claims to the general partner's personal assets in the event of a default (Cole 2008). It is expected that smaller banks would lend mostly to proprietors and partnerships while large banks will lend mostly to larger firms and corporations. This therefore seems to indicate precisely the existence of correlation with size.

4.1.6   Nature of Business of Firm's Industrial Sector

Anecdotal evidence shows that a "firm's sector of activity or industrial classification is often used by bankers to evaluate a firm's credit quality" (Cole 1998: 964). In other words, bankers presume that there are certain sectors or industries where the borrowers are less likely to default on a loan. If this is the case, banks may withdraw from funding certain other sectors even when they are faced with financial difficulties. A firm's industrial classification could also give an indication of the type and maturity of the financing source[1] it requires. Typically, high-growth

---

[1]Research has shown positive relationships between the use of long-term debt and sectors such as retail, distribution, hotel, catering and 'other manufacturing' sectors (Bhaird 2010: 63).

and non-high growth firms attract different funding preferences from lenders. For example, small firms in the computer and software development and services sector or firms that invest hugely on R&D are seen as high-growth firms. High growth firms usually do not have adequate internal finance to fulfil their business needs and are therefore prone to raising external finance. It is contended that though large banks are generally less attracted to small businesses, they however prefer to lend to small hi-tech and super-growth[2] firms.

4.1.7   Firm's Credit Rating

A firm's credit rating, as determined by previous loan repayments or number of delinquencies is a crucial factor in influencing a lender's decision. Number of delinquencies is the number of business credit obligations on which the firm has been delinquent within the past three years. Business delinquencies are a negative function of the likelihood that a lender will extend credit to the firm (Cole 1998, 2008; Cole et al. 2004).

4.2   Owner Characteristics

The literature shows that the decision of banks to grant credit to small businesses is also largely dependent on the reputation of the owners as measured by their age, educational attainment, business experience, physiological characteristics (e.g. race, ethnicity, gender), personal wealth and delinquencies.

4.2.1   Owner/Entrepreneur's Credit Rating

Business owners or entrepreneurs with bad credit history will find it more difficult to obtain working capital loans. An entrepreneur's credit rating can be measured by *number of delinquencies*. This represents the number of personal credit obligations on which the principal owner has been 60 or more days delinquent. Banks should be less inclined to lend to firms whose owners have had a great deal of delinquencies (e.g. Cole 1998, 2008; Cole et al. 2004).

---

[2]Super-growth firms refer to firms that have consistently high growth rates and whose annual growth rates are in excess of 30 % (See 2007 Survey of SME finance by Cosh et al. 2008).

4.2.2 Owners' Educational Attainment

This is measured by *academic qualifications or other professional training* and usually takes the following order: high school, college degree, graduate degree or post-graduate degree. Firms with more educated owners are thought of to be credit worthy as they will bring their knowledge and skills to bear on the fortunes of the company. In an empirical study by MacRae (1991), it was found that the major distinguishing feature between high growth and low growth small firms was the education, training and experience of the senior managers and owners. Small firm owners with strong managerial competences are also likely to attract, develop and retain workforce with strong managerial talent (Martin and Staines 1994) and this would impact on the company's financial performance.

4.2.3 Owners' Business Experience

The quality of the human capital of the people working in the SME is a critical factor influencing the likelihood that the business is able to grow successfully (Dess and Picken 1999). Firms with more experienced owners are thus generally assumed to be more credit worthy than younger entrepreneurs because of their expertise in the firm's area of business. In a survey of Scottish bank managers on their lending practices to small businesses, Fletcher (1995) found that trading experience of the borrower is rated the most important factor for lending to small businesses. In order for lending officers to be able to extend credit on a particular project, they will need to ascertain that a borrower has the capability and a positive track record of successfully managing a similar project in the past or a project that requires comparable competence, know-how and technical skills to the new project under consideration (Bruns and Fletcher 2008). Borrowers that are able to demonstrate competence or a positive track record are likely to get a favourable decision from the lending officers (Sargent and Young 1991; Scherr et al. 1993).

4.2.4 Owner's Equity Stake/Contribution

According to Bruns and Fletcher (2008), the probability that a lending officer will support credit extension to a borrower will depend on the share of the investment the owner has in the borrowing firm. Due to the combined role of management and ownership, the owner-manager has both financial and human capital at risk in the firm. Lenders sometimes require small business borrowers to make cash contribution of a certain percentage of the loan amount, so the borrowers can demonstrate that they will act in the lender's best interest. Mishkin (2010: 184) calls a debt contract of this nature "incentive compatible", i.e. where the borrower's incentive is aligned with that of the lender. Equity stake is important from the point of view of gearing and showing commitment by the owner (Fletcher 1995). Equity stake suggests that the track record of the owner(s) of the business is critical as an indication that they have the ability to utilize the loan for the purpose for which it was initially contracted.

4.2.5   Owner's Personal Wealth

The wealth of firm owners is likely to play a key role in determining the allocation of credit to small firms where personal commitments are pre-requisites for obtaining credit, i.e. where borrowers pledge their personal assets as collateral against the firm's borrowings and/or make personal guarantees in order to be able to reduce the risk of lending (Avery et al. 1998). Owners with greater personal assets and higher income should be able to negotiate credit terms better as they can demonstrate good prospects to the bankers or sufficient ability to repay a loan.

4.2.6   Owner's Physical/Social Characteristics (e.g. Age, Gender, Race, and Nationality)

Firms with older owners are usually thought of to be wiser and to have more experience or track record of credit-related transactions than young owners and are therefore more likely to be given preference. Some bankers are also gender-bias in their lending practices. Firms whose controlling owners are female usually face more stringent credit requirements than males (e.g. Bellucci et al. 2009). Owners' race/ethnicity is also a very important factor in assessing banks that practice race-based discrimination. The victims are usually loan applicants from minority ethnic groups such as Black Africans, Hispanics and Asians (e.g. Blanchard et al. 2008). In fact, using data from the 1993 and 1998 National Surveys of Small Business Finances to examine the existence of racial discrimination in the small business credit market, Blanchflower et al. (2003) find that black-owned small businesses are about twice as likely to be denied credit even after controlling for differences in creditworthiness and other factors.

4.3   Firm-Lender Relationship Characteristics

The borrowers' chances of accessing bank finance are partly dependent on the existence of previous relationship with the lender. This sub-section examines how credit is constrained by the existence or non-existence of prior relationships with the lender as well as the strength of such relationships. Firms that have pre-existing relationships with their prospective lenders are likely to be favoured to receive credit because it is expected that over the course of these relationships, the lender would have garnered sufficient information about the credit worthiness of the borrower. Cole et al. (2004) identify three types of pre-existing relationships.

4.3.1   Deposit Relationship

It is expected that banks should favour firms that have a pre-existing deposit account (checking or savings) at the bank. Nakamura (1994) and Boot (2000) note that through the checking and savings account information of local customers, banks are able to ascertain the credit worthiness of their loan applicants. Cole et al. (2004) also notes that banks would most likely grant loan requests made by firms with pre-existing deposit relationships for fear of losing them to their competitors because of the loan denial.

4.3.2   Loan Relationship

The lender is likely to favour applicants that have had a pre-existing loan relationship with the bank. However, the effect of this relationship is rather ambiguous. This is because the lender might be worried that a pre-existing loan clearly increases the firm's leverage, *ceteris paribus* (Cole 1998). In addition, if a bank grants a second loan application to a borrower, it might signal concerns about the bank's portfolio diversification and a possible violation of regulatory restrictions on lending to a single borrower.

4.3.3   Financial Management Relationship

Like deposit relationship, it is expected that a firm with a pre-existing financial management relationship with the bank will have greater chances of receiving a loan. Financial management services used by SMEs include *transaction services* (the provision of paper money and coins, credit card and debit card processing, night depository, and wire transfers); *cash management services* (i.e. the provision of liquid asset and interest-bearing accounts), and *credit-related services* (including the provision of loans, trade credit and capital leases; letters of credit, bankers' acceptances and factoring). Other financial management services include *brokerage and trust services* (pensions, business trusts and safe keeping of securities (Elliehausen and Wolken 1990; Cole 1998; Mach and Wolken 2006). These services are typical of all types of banks. However, one would expect applicants to larger banks to have had a pre-existing financial management relationship.

Even if a relationship exists between the borrower and the lender, the strength of that relationship is also crucial in determining whether a borrower will get a loan or not. For the purpose of this analysis, the strength of a borrower-lender relationship will be measured by the following factors:

4.3.4   The Length and Exclusivity of Relationship

The length of a firm-bank relationship and the number of sources of financial services a borrower deals with are important determinants of credit decisions. The longer the relationship between a firm and a lender, the more time the potential lender has to acquire and develop proprietary information about the applicant (Cole 1998). Large banking institutions are found to have temporarily shorter and less exclusive relationships with their business customers (e.g. Berger et al. 2005a, b) owing mainly to competition from other financial service providers. Because large banks tend to have weaker relationships with borrowers, they tend to employ more transactions lending approaches. On the contrary, the relationship between banks and firms tend to be long-lived and more exclusive when the firm in consideration borrows from a small bank. This confirms the assertion made by Rajan (1992) that small firms tend to be tied to banks that have accumulated soft information on them over time. The reason why small firms are unlikely to switch banks is that soft information is exclusive to the bank they are dealing with and as such is not easily transferable across banks. On the other hand, a firm dealing with a large bank is likely to find that the additional benefits of staying with the same bank or the costs of switching to another lender is low (Berger et al. 2005a, b: 245). However, it could be argued that this might not be the case if the firm is considerably small.

4.3.5   Distance[3] and Mode of Interaction[4]

Large banks tend to develop more impersonal and longer distance relationships with their SME loan customers. This is consistent with the view that large banks rely less on soft information that is acquired mainly through personal contact with customers and by observation. Berger et al. (2005a, b: 240). By contrast, because

---

[3]Distance refers to the physical (linear) space between the applicant firm's address and the address of the bank branch with which the firm trades.

[4]Mode of interaction can be classified into personal and impersonal. Personal Interaction is simply characterised by the banker's face-to-face contact with the customer, while impersonal contact is characterised by a greater use of mails and phone calls in communications instead of face-to-face contact.

small banks deal with informationally opaque firms, they tend to more susceptible to the "*shoe-leather*" cost of personal visits (ibid: 245). However, the fact that large banks deal with customers at an impersonal level does not imply that they are incompetent in dealing more at a personal level, but because the nature of the firms they deal with makes personal contact unsuitable.

4.3.6   Effects of Relationships on the Availability of Credit

So far, it has been argued that banks that are able to build stronger and lengthier relationships with small firms are better able to acquire soft information, which then helps them to assess the credit worthiness of borrowers. But how do these stronger relationships translate into more financing? The problem of measuring the availability of credit cannot be easily ascertained from the books of small firms, as this might reveal a combination of both demand and supply side effects. However, Petersen and Rajan (1994) suggest an alternative approach whereby the degree to which a firm relies on trade credit can be used to ascertain the extent to which it has been credit constrained and hence gives a signal on the firm's source of bank finance. Under this model, if a firm pays a greater proportion of its trade credit late (that is, after the due date), it gives a reliable indication that the firm in question might have been rationed so that we conclude that the firm must have borrowed from a large bank. In other words, since credit rationing among informationally opaque firms increases as bank size increases, it is expected that a small firm that borrows from a large bank will be more prone to credit rationing. Older and larger firms are arguably less constrained by banks and hence are likely to pay less of their trade credit late. In the same vein, firms that have built long-term relationships with their banks are also likely to pay less of their trade credit late (Berger et al. 2005a, b: 260).

4.4   Demand Side Market Failures

There are also market failures affecting the demand side for businesses seeking finance. These come in the following forms:

4.4.1   Availability of Marketable Collateral

The use of collateral is a common feature of loan contracts between firms and lenders. Collateral requirements either in the form of business or personal assets are used to reduce the risk of lending which is caused by the presence of asymmetric information, adverse selection and moral hazard. In collateralised lending, the borrower undertakes to relinquish ownership of a valuable asset to the lender if he or she fails to repay a loan. If the borrower defaults on the loan, the lender reserves the right to seize, sell or liquidate the asset and use the proceeds to offset the loan. Nakamura (1994: 8) argues that, "because the lender has recourse to the collateral, the borrower has a strong incentive to repay the loan in full[5]". In this sense, according to Voordeckers and Steijvers (2006), collateral may play a disciplinary role in the behaviour of the borrower. But most small business borrowers, especially young and inexperienced firms with low credit quality, do not have access to acceptable forms of collateral, such as real estate, cash and other liquid assets. As part of efforts to solve this problem in the UK, the UK government introduced the *Enterprise Finance Guarantee Scheme (EFG)* in January 2009 to provide a 75 % guarantee on individual loans made by participating banks to small companies with turnover less than £25 million.

4.4.2   Strength of Borrowers' Balance Sheet

During a recession, slow down in lending levels could be explained by the generally weak state of borrowers' balance sheets (Bernanke and Lown 1991). For example, many borrowers significantly increased their leverage during the few years prior to the build up of the recent crises, while falling prices for real estate and other assets have adversely affected potential borrowers' net worth. Further, the recession has put additional pressures on cash flows. For a given set of ultimate investment opportunities, borrowers who are less creditworthy (such as those who have higher leverage or lower collateral) will have a lower effective demand for external finance at given values of the safe real interest rate. Thus, it may be that in the recent downturn the normal recessionary decline in credit demand has been exacerbated by a greater-than-normal decline in the creditworthiness of potential borrowers.

4.4.3   Information Market Failures

There are information market failures affecting the demand side for businesses seeking finance. SMEs may not fully understand the potential benefits to their business of raising finance or their likely chance of success in gaining finance, which ultimately means they do not apply for finance. This may restrict the growth

---

[5]However, it should be noted that that there are huge transaction costs involved with administering the sale of a collateralised property. Moreover, in some cases the value of the collateral may have diminished beyond the amount borrowed. Thus the gains to the lender might be unobtrusive (Cole et al. 2004).

of businesses. Survey evidence shows a small but significant proportion of SMEs are discouraged from applying for finance because they think they will be rejected (BIS 2012). The November 2011 SME Finance Monitor survey in the UK estimates around 40 % of would be seekers (12 % of all SMEs) are discouraged, and this is equivalent to around 5 % of all SMEs that are discouraged from applying for external finance (BDRC Continental 2011).

4.4.4   Business Confidence

A lack of investment readiness also leads to SMEs lacking the ability to present themselves as investable opportunities, for instance due to *inadequate management skills* or *poor business plans* (BIS 2012). For instance, according to the 2011 SME Finance Monitor, only 25 % of SMEs in the UK have a formally qualified financial manager, although this increases with the size of business to 66 % of medium sized businesses (BDRC Continental 2011). This may reflect why 41 % of SME employers do not understand the way banks assess business credit risk, and why they do not feel confident in raising finance. A greater number of SME employers perceive they are poor (38 %) at accessing finance compared to those reporting they are strong (25 %). However, most SMEs do not seek advice when applying for finance, with only 9 % of SMEs seeking advice when applying an overdraft and 20 % of SMEs seeking advice when applying for a loan (BDRC Continental 2011).

4.4.5   Poor Quality of Projects

Another similar 'demand side' constraint has to do with the quality of projects submitted for financing, which often falls short of the minimum standards. It is worth mentioning, however, that the poor quality of projects is frequently invoked as an excuse by conservative bankers not to extend lending to SMEs (Zavatta 2008). Although it is not easy to come by potentially viable projects, the issue of the quality of projects is a problem of perception.

4.4.6   Inability to Exploit Existing Opportunities

Notwithstanding the intrinsic quality of the projects being considered for financing, bankers are also concerned that business promoters are often unable to make the best use of available opportunities. This relates not only to their limited ability to convincingly articulate their business ideas, but also to the unwillingness of many small-scale entrepreneurs to 'waste time' in dealing with financial institutions (Zavatta 2008). Sometimes, business owners are unwilling to commit to building a strong relationship with bankers unless their business proposals are first considered for financing. In fact, many small businesses often quickly consider the option of switching to other financial service providers once they are unsatisfied with the level of funding they get from their existing bankers. The costs of switching to other financial service providers is, however, huge, when considering the extent of proprietary information that has been acquired by the bankers over time as well as the costs of building new relationships with new financial service providers.

References

Altman EI (1968) Financial ratios, discriminant analysis and the prediction of corporate bankruptcy. J Finance 23(4):589–609

Altman EI (1993) Corporate financial distress and bankruptcy: a complete guide to predicting and avoiding distress and profiting from bankruptcy, 2nd edn. Wiley, New York

Avery RB, Bostic RW, Samolyk KA (1998) The role of personal wealth in small business finance. J Bank Finance 22:1019–1061

Barrett GR (1990) What bankers want to know before granting a small business loan. J Account 169(4):47–54

Beaver W (1967) "Financial ratios as predictors of failure" empirical research in accounting: selected studies 1966. J Account Res 4:71–111

Behr P, Guttler A (2007) Credit risk assessment and relationship lending: an empirical analysis of German small and medium-sized enterprises. J Small Bus Manage 45(2):194–213

Bellucci A, Borisov AV, Zazzaro A (2009) Does gender matter in bank-firm relationships? Evidence from small business lending. Money and Finance Research Group (MoFiR) Working Paper No. 31

Berger AN, Udell GF (2003) Small business and debt finance". In: Acs ZJ, Audretsch DB (eds) Handbook of entrepreneurship research. Kluver Academic Publishers, Great Britain, pp 299–328

Berger AN, Udell GF (2006) A more complete conceptual framework for financing of small and medium enterprises. J Finance Bank 30(11):2945–2966

Berger AN, Miller NH, Petersen MA, Rajan RG, Stein JC (2005a) Does function follow organisational form? Evidence from the lending practices of large and small banks. J Financ Econ 76:237–269

Berger A, Frame WS, Miller NH (2005b) Credit scoring and the availability, price and risk of small business credit. J Money Credit Bank 37:191–222

Berkowitz J, White MJ (2004) Bankruptcy and small firms' access to credit. RAND J Econ 35 (1):69–84

Bernanke BS, Lown CS (1991) the credit crunch. Brookings Pap Econ Act 2:205–247

Berry AJ, Faulkner S, Hughes M, Jarvis R (1993) Financial information, the banker and the small business. Br Account Rev 25:131–150

Bhaird C (2010) Resourcing small and medium sized enterprises: a financial growth life cycle approach. Contributions to management science seriesSpringer, Berlin, p 210

Blanchard L, Zhao B, Yinger J (2008) Do lenders discriminate against minority and woman entrepreneurs? J Urban Econ 63:467–497

Blanchflower DG, Levine PB, Zimmerman DJ (2003) Discrimination in the small-business credit market. Rev Econ Stat 85(4):930–943

Boot AWA (2000) Relationship banking: what do we know? J Financ Intermediation 9:7–25

Bruns V, Fletcher M (2008) Banks' risk assessment of Swedish SMEs. Venture Capital 10 (2):171–194

Cole R (1998) The importance of relationships to the availability of credit. J Bank Finance 22:959–997

Cole R (2008) Who needs credit and who gets credit? Evidence from the surveys of small business finances, MPRA Paper No 24691

Cole RA, Goldberg LG, White LJ (2004) Cookie-cutter versus character: the micro structure of small business lending by large and small banks. J Financ Quant Anal 39(2):227–251

BDRC Continental (2011) SME finance monitor survey. Available at: http://bdrc-continental.com/wp-content/uploads/2014/11/Q3-2011-SME-Finance-Monitor.pdf. Last Accessed 11 Feb 2015

Cosh A, Hughes A, Bullock A, Milner I (2008) Financing UK small and medium enterprises: the 2007 survey. A report from the Centre for Business Research (CBR)

Department for Business Innovation and Skills (2012) "SME access to external finance. BIS Economics Paper No. 16. Available at: https://www.gov.uk/government/uploads/system/uploads/attachment_data/file/32263/12-539-sme-access-external-finance.pdf. Last Accessed 11 Feb 2015

Dess GG, Picken HC (1999) Beyond productivity: how leading companies achieve superior performance by leveraging their human capital. American Management Association, New York, p 244

Dewhurst J, Burns P (1989) Small business: planning, finance and control, 2nd edn. Palgrave Macmillan, London, p 392

Elliehausen GE, Wolken JD (1990) Banking markets and the use of financial services by small and medium-sized businesses. Fed Res Bull Staff Stud 160

Fletcher M (1995) Decision making by scottish bank managers. Int J Entrepreneurial Behav Res 1 (2):37–53

Haynes GW, Ou C, Berney R (1999) Small business borrowing from large and small banks. In: Blanton JL, Williams A, Rhine SLW (eds) Business access to capital and credit. A federal reserve system research conference, pp 287–327

Hutchinson RW, McKillop DG (1992) Banks and small to medium size business financing in the United Kingdom: some general issues. Nat Westminster Bank Q Rev 84–95

Hyytinen A, Pajarinen M (2008) Opacity of young businesses: Evidence from rating disagreements. J Bank Finance 32:1234–1241

Kam V (1990) Accounting theory, 2nd edn. Wiley, Singapore, p 608

Kim NJ (2008) 'Financial statements and loan decision in community banks. Int Rev Bus Res Pap 4(4):199–207

Mach TL, Wolken JD (2006) Financial services used by small businesses: evidence from the 2003 survey of small business finance. Fed Res Bull A167–A195

MacRae D (1991) Characteristics of high and low growth small and medium-sized businesses. Paper presented to 21st European small business seminar, Barcelona

Martin G, Staines H (1994) Managerial competences in small firms. J Manage Dev 13(7):23–24

Mishkin FS (2010) The economics of money, banking and financial markets, 9th edn. Pearson, London, p 664

Nakamura, LI (1994) Small borrowers and the survival of the small bank: is mouse bank Mighty or Mickey? Federal Reserve Bank of Philadelphia Business Review 3–15

Ohlson JA (1980) Financial ratios and the probabilistic prediction of bankruptcy. J Account Res 18:109–131

Petersen MA, Rajan RG (1994) The benefits of firm-creditor relationships: Evidence from small business data. J Finance 49:3–37

Rajan RG (1992) Insiders and outsiders: the choice between informed and arm's-length debt. J Finance 47:1367–1400

Sargent M, Young JE (1991) The entrepreneurial search for capital: a behavioural science perspective. Entrepreneurship Reg Dev 3:237–252

Scherr FC, Sugrue TF, Ward JB (1993) Financing the small firm start-up: determinants of debt use. J Small Bus Finance 3(1):17–36

Voordeckers W, Steijvers T (2006) Business collateral and personal commitments in SME lending. J Bank Finance 30:3067–3086

Zavatta R (2008) Financing technology entrepreneurs and SMEs in developing countries. infoDev/World Bank, Washington, DC

Chapter 5
Supply-Side Factors Affecting Bank Lending to SMEs

Supply side behaviour towards small business lending is mostly driven by (1) *the risk and cost factors associated with lending activity*, (2) *financial institution and market structure*, (3) *the lending technology*, and (4) *the lending infrastructure*.

5.1 Risk and Cost Factors

5.1.1 Cost of Funds

Changes in the bank's capital or balance sheet liquidity might affect cost of funds to borrowers. In order to lend money to businesses, banks need to attract funds (e.g. bank capital, deposit liabilities, or wholesale funds) by paying a return or interest on them. According to the loanable funds theory, banks need to aim to hold deposits for similar lengths of time as the term of loans financed. In order to survive, banks have to cover the interest rates they pay on deposits from interest rates they charge on loans (interest margin). Higher loan prices in turn affect the quantity of funds intermediated by banks. Hubbard et al. (2002) investigated the effects of banks' financial condition on the borrowers' cost of funds after controlling for borrower risk and information costs. They find that capital-constrained banks charge higher loan rates than well-capitalised banks and that this cost difference is especially associated with borrowers for which 'information costs' and 'incentive problems' are most important (p. 561). Their result is also consistent with models that allow banks to charge a risk premium to borrowers facing switching costs in bank-borrower relationships, as well as models of the bank-lending channel of monetary transmission.

5.1.2 Informational Asymmetries

As noted earlier in Sect. 2.2, informational asymmetries are always present in enterprise financing transactions. Entrepreneurs typically possess privileged

© The Author(s) 2016
V.U. Ekpu, *Determinants of Bank Involvement with SMEs*,
SpringerBriefs in Finance, DOI 10.1007/978-3-319-25837-9_5

information on their businesses that cannot be easily accessed—or cannot be accessed at all—by prospective lenders. According to the New Keynesians, this leads to two problems. First, the lender/investor may not be able to differentiate adequately between 'high quality' and 'low quality' companies and projects. In that case, price variables (i.e. interest rates) may not work well as a screening device, because high interests may lead to an excessively risky portfolio (the 'adverse selection' problem). Second, once the lenders/investors have supplied the funding, they may not be able to assess whether the enterprise is utilizing the funds in an appropriate manner (the 'moral hazard' problem). To mitigate these problems, bankers may adopt precautionary measures, such as requiring that financing be collateralized. Alternatively, they may simply turn down the request for financing ('credit rationing'). Informational asymmetries tend to pose more severe problems for SMEs than for larger business. The information that SME can realistically provide to external financiers (in the form of financial accounts, business plans, feasibility studies, etc.) often lacks detail and rigor. This problem is often aggravated by the low level of education of small entrepreneurs, who may not be in the position to adequately articulate their case.

5.1.3   Lenders' Risk Appetite

Following from Post Keynesian view of lenders behaviour, banks are only willing to lend to borrowers when the risk/return profile of such borrowers are in their favour (Coppola 2014). Risk appetite is simply the extent to which a lender is willing or inclined to finance a borrower. It is usually measured as *positive, negative* or *neutral*. Risk appetite is shaped by a number of factors: *history of previous loan performance, risk profile of business sectors being financed, amount of loan security, financial regulations* and *general economic and financial conditions*. The amount and price of credit supplied to a borrower reflect, according to the banks' experience and its loan performance data, the probability of the borrower not being able to repay the debt. The higher the level of risk, the higher the price must be to cover the likely loss. Banks are now more risk averse, both due to the credit crunch and because they are required to be compliant with new financial services regulations (e.g. Basel III). These new rules require banks to hold more capital against certain types of assets. For every loan a bank makes, it must set capital aside to cover for unexpected losses. The idea is to ensure the bank remains solvent and depositors are secure, even if that loan becomes impaired. In order to protect depositors from losses and reinforce consumer confidence in the banking sector, all banks around the world are currently holding higher levels of capital than in recent years. There is a cost to holding this capital and, as banks have increased the amount set aside, this cost has risen along with it.

The amount of risk a bank is faced with is also influenced by the level of security offered by the borrower, so that when the value of security falls, such as commercial property values, the risk increases, and vice versa. The Basel III regulatory framework sets the methodology and calculations used to determine the cost associated with the risk of lending. Risk-adjusted loan pricing enables higher-risk but still allows viable businesses to access finance whilst lower-risk and well-managed firms get the benefit of lower-cost funding. Pricing of risk is in the interest of businesses; even more marginal businesses can still get access to finance (BBA 2011).

5.1.4 Transaction Costs

Besides risk profile considerations, the business of lending to SMEs is associated with several transaction costs (e.g. Zavatta 2008; Duan et al. 2009; Venkatesh and Kumari 2011). These include: (i) *administrative costs* (e.g. costs of meeting a business customer, appraising a loan application and conducting due diligence, setting up a facility, monitoring, controlling, and revising that facility, etc.); (ii) *legal fees* (e.g. costs of providing the legal or contract documentation, filing debt claims, etc.); and (iii) *costs related to the acquisition and dissemination of information* (e.g. costs of purchasing a credit profile from a specialized agency and costs of disseminating regular information such as notification of interest rate changes or changes to other lending fees). While banks may use credit and performance-scoring tools, most lending decisions will also require a judgment to be made by an experienced relationship manager. Because of their size, smaller facilities tend to have a relatively higher transaction cost per pound lent than larger facilities, and not all of that cost can be recovered through fees. So small facilities tend to bear higher margins, even if the risk is comparable with larger lending.

5.2 Financial Institution and Market Structure

5.2.1 Bank Size and Organizational Structure

Credit supply to SMEs is also constrained by the banks' organizational structure in terms of the decision making strategy vis-à-vis the administration of lending functions: appraising and approving loan applications, monitoring of credit risks, reviewing loan performance, etc. Differences in bank organization structure account for the operational differences that exist in the loan approval processes of banks. The operational differences between banks of different sizes can be better understood within the framework of Williamson's (1967) theory of hierarchical control. As the size of an organization increases, it loses control between successive hierarchies because of its centralized decision making structure. Large banks therefore tend to follow explicit rules and procedures in order to avoid distortions, which tend to arise in a multiple layer structure. Small banks on the other hand may be able to give greater discretion to their loan officers because of their fewer layers of management and decentralized structure. Similarly, as large banks expand in size and geography (i.e. number of branches), it becomes difficult to monitor the behaviour of employees and this could lead to agency problems. In order to maintain control, large banks must establish formal lending procedures, which all staff should follow (Cole et al. 2004).

Although large banks tend to enjoy economies of scale in processing hard information, they are relatively fraught with organizational diseconomies[1] with respect to processing soft information because it is difficult to quantify relationships and transmit them through the channels of communication prevalent in large organizations (e.g. Stein 2002; Berger and Udell 2006). For example, under relationship banking, large banks with a multi-branch hierarchy face agency problems. This is because it may be difficult for a relationship manager who is the custodian of soft information to communicate same to the management or owners of the bank. Thus this may give relative advantage in relationship banking to small institutions because they typically have fewer intermediaries between ownership and management. This means that because small institutions have lower agency costs in the sense that there is only a thin line of separation between ownership and management, they are more likely to have comparative advantage over their large multi-office counterparts in the financing of SMEs using relationship-lending techniques.

5.2.2 Ownership Structure

Apart from size considerations, the lending practices of banks and their willingness to lend to SMEs are also largely correlated with the type of ownership structure of the lender. For example, conventional wisdom with regard to small business financing says that small domestic private banks are more likely to finance SMEs because they are better suited to utilizing 'relationship lending' approaches based on the acquisition of soft information by the loan officer through continuous, personalized, direct contacts with SMEs, their promoters and the local business community in which they operate (e.g. Berger and Udell 1995; Keeton 1995, and Strahan and Weston 1998). However, some recent studies (e.g. Berger and Udell 2006; Berger et al. 2007, and De la Torre et al. 2010) have begun to dispute this conventional wisdom and propose a new paradigm for bank SME finance, arguing that large and foreign banks can be as effective in SME lending through transactions lending technologies (e.g. credit scoring, asset based lending, factoring, leasing, etc.) and centralized structures instead of relationship lending. In yet another recent

---

[1]Organisational diseconomies in large firms can also be explained by the fact that large firms, especially those created by consolidation are efficient in financing transactions loans and offering wholesale services to large corporate customers making them reduce the provision of retail services to small firms (see for example, Williamson 1967, 1988; Stein 2002; Berger and Udell 2006).

study, Beck et al. (2011) find that foreign, domestic, private and government owned banks use different lending technologies and organizational structures for SME financing. However, they find that the extent, type and pricing of SME loans are not strongly correlated with lending technologies and organizational structures; suggesting that lending technologies are somewhat irrelevant in issues of SME financing.

5.2.3   Effect of Bank Consolidation

The global consolidation in the banking industry has raised concerns about the survivability of small banks, and as small banks are vital sources of credit for small firms, these concerns become more important for the survival of the economy as a whole. The most compelling evidence from numerous studies (especially for US) reveal that large banking institutions tend to reduce their small business lending after mergers and acquisitions. However, this reduction appears to be offset at least in part by the decision of other banks in the same local market (de novo banks) to substantially increase lending to small businesses by way of response. (e.g. Peek and Rosengren 1995a; Berger et al. 1998; Avery and Samolyk 2004). But recent results shown in Schmieder et al. (2010) appear to be intriguing as the authors found that consolidation does not have a sustainable negative impact on the financing of SMEs in the German market. One reason alluded for this is the absence of a "negative size effect" as well as the efficiency and competitiveness of the German banking market, which reduces any potential threats to SME financing (p. 464). This perhaps also suggests that the nature of the German financial system (being a bank-based system) has positive effects on the financing of small businesses. Strahan and Weston (1998) investigated the case of consolidation among small independent banks in USA and found a positive impact on small business lending. However, for small banks that are members of a bank holding company (BHC), results show that they tend to replicate the behaviour of their parent companies, implying that they lend less to small businesses (Keeton 1995; Jayaratne and Wolken 1999).

One crucial matter in considering the effect of consolidation on small business lending is the issue of *motives* of the acquirer bank. Accordingly, if a large bank acquires a smaller bank because it is mainly interested in acquiring low-cost deposits or in expanding its geographic market reach, then there is likelihood that it might restrain its lending to small businesses (Peek and Rosengren 1995a). Furthermore, an acquirer bank might find that rather than manage risks locally, it will be more profitable to manage its liquidity and loan diversification more efficiently on a larger scale. On the other hand, a large bank might be attracted by a small bank's profitable small business loan portfolio. In that case, the large bank might be strongly incentivized to maintain existing borrowing relationships. Hence it might want to support an even greater level of small business lending (Levonian and Soller 1996).

Mergers and acquisition also have an *effect on loan pricing*. Rauch and Hendrickson (2004) found that, *all else being equal*, consolidation lowers the interest rates charged by large banks for small business borrowers who qualify, while small banks raise the loan rates for borrowers who do not. One of the factors that determine the post merger loan spreads in banks is the operational efficiency of the enlarged group. Erel (2006) supports this argument and finds that mergers reduce loan spreads, especially when there are huge cost savings from the reduction in post merger operating expenses and that this result is stronger when the acquirer bank and the target bank have some market overlaps. However, there might be fears that significant in-market overlaps could raise loan spreads and create more concerns for market power. As the size and complexity of organization increases, organizational diseconomies might set in as costs of small business lending rises in the enlarged institution (Strahan and Weston 1998; Stein 2002). There is also considerable evidence that even small banks' acquisition of soft information about borrowers reduces after a merger (e.g. Ogura and Uchida 2007). This view is consistent with Stein's (2002) prediction that organizations with a relatively flatter structure are likely to perform better in acquiring soft information. Cavallo and Rossi (2001) also suggest that mergers should be oriented towards raising the scope for small banks to expand their scale of production while enabling large banks to improve efficiency by focusing on output mix diversification.

5.2.4 Effect of Bank Market Structure and Competition

Firms' access to bank finance is also constrained by the bank market structure, i.e. the level of competition and concentration in the bank market. Some studies find that higher concentration is associated with higher credit availability, which is consistent with the *information hypothesis* that less competitive banks have more incentive to invest in soft information. Other empirical studies, however, find support for the *market power hypothesis* that credit rationing is higher in less competitive bank markets (Carbo-Valverde et al. 2009). Market structure effects on credit availability occur in at least two ways: product market competition and regional or geographic market competition.

Product Market Competition: Product market competition can be explained in terms of the size of loan as well as the range of financial services banks can offer their customers. Larger banks are generally able to make larger loans than smaller relationship-driven banks. Because there are fixed costs associated with processing and monitoring any size of loan, larger banks benefit from scale economies when they make large loans. They are also able to benefit from scale economies by using credit scoring to make large amounts of standardized loans and credit cards to businesses. Large and foreign banks are also able to offer certain types of financial services to their customers to generate additional fee income, such as foreign exchange transactions, interest rate swaps, asset financing, commercial papers, bankers' acceptances, and so on.

Geographic or Regional Market Competition: Lending to small businesses can also be influenced by the population density, competition and nature of economic activity in the local area being served or where small business customers carry out their primary trading activities. Large banks tend to situate their offices in areas of relatively high population density and where there is a substantial amount of economic activity, while small banks generally have higher market share in the rural areas due to the nature of their small business customers. But Gilbert (2000a, b) reports that the trends have since changed as he finds evidence that large banks are gaining increasing interest and market share in small business lending in many rural communities in US including relatively low population density areas.

Since the 1980s and early 1990s, increasing bank deregulation (namely the relaxation of controls or constraints over the scale and scope of banking business[2]) has led to geographic branch expansion by large banks across borders. Large banks especially are now able to make distant loans to business customers, thanks to credit scoring and other transactions lending approaches. However, such automated loans have certain limits[3] beyond which the decision is taken on the basis of other factors as decided by the relationship managers and credit risk sanctioners. Critics of multi-office banks have argued that the lending behaviour of large banks does not support small business lending (Keeton 1995). First, because of their size, large banks might have incentives to make more of large loans and less of small loans. Second, large banks follow rigid lending rules due to their centralised organisational structure. This might discourage relationship lending and hence result in fewer loans being granted to small businesses. Lastly, large banks are assumed to use deposits acquired through their multi-office branches to finance large institutional or cross border investments.

5.2.5 The Profitability Incentive

Banks' supply of loans to SMEs is largely driven by their perception of the size and profitability of the SME lending market. In fact, in a survey of lenders, 81 % of banks in developed countries and 72 % of banks in developing countries indicate that profitability is the most important determinant of their involvement with SMEs (Beck et al. 2008). In a similar survey of bankers' view of lending relationships by Bharath et al. (2007), many bankers view the generation of additional business in the future as the principal reason for engaging in relationship lending. In fact, this search for yield contributed to the apparent replacement of traditional business lending with securitization of bank loans during the build-up to the recent financial

---

[2]In US, the Riegel-Neal Interstate Banking and Branching Efficiency Act of 1994 removed restrictions on nationwide branching since June 1997 and permitted bank holding companies to buy existing banks and other holding companies located throughout the nation beginning from the fall of 1995 (Gilbert 2000a, b).

[3]In RBS for example, this limit is £25,000.

crisis. Prior to the crisis, banks were regularly initiating loans with the intention of selling off all or part of their holdings to other investors. Loans that are securitized in this manner do not appear on banks' balance sheets and thus would not be counted in standard measures of bank loans (Bernanke and Lown 1991).

5.3 Lending Technology

Generally, SME lenders use a variety of lending technologies to resolve the problems of informational opacity associated with small firms. The main categories are 'relationship driven' technologies, and 'transactions driven' technologies (Berger and Udell 1995, 2003, 2006; Stein 2002). Relationship banking is a very popular term in the banking literature and it refers to the provision of financial services by a financial intermediary that invests largely in acquiring 'customer-specific information', especially of a 'proprietary[4] nature' and adds to this body of private information through 'multiple interactions with the same customer over time and/or across products' (Boot 2000:10) as well as through the local community in which the customer operates. Banks obtain proprietary information often through *screening* and they consolidate the information gathered over time as they appraise the profitability of their clients' investments through *monitoring* (i.e. multiple interactions). On the other hand, transactions driven banking tend to provide *arms-length* finance and focuses on one transaction rather than emphasizing continuous information gathering across multiple transactions and across time. Because asymmetric information is relatively more associated with small businesses than large businesses, majority of banks, especially large ones have resorted to the use of impersonal[5] approaches in lending to small businesses. This is especially the case because most large banks use transactions lending technologies[6] in lending to small businesses.

In advanced credit markets, the processing of information is mostly done electronically using a type of transactions lending technique called credit-scoring models. In many low and middle income countries where the credit system is still underdeveloped, banks rely hugely on traditional relationship lending, i.e. the use of qualitative assessment based on the 5Cs of lending—*character*, *capacity*,·

---

[4]Proprietary information refers to information that is privy to only the financial intermediary and the customer.

[5]Impersonal lending approaches refer mostly to those lending practices, which support lending at a distance because of certain characteristics of the small business borrower or his firm. Such lending practices might involve more of the use of mail or telephone conversations rather than frequent personal visits to the bank as small banks do (see Berger et al. 2005).

[6]Examples of transactions lending technologies include financial statement lending; asset based lending, credit scoring, trade credit, and factoring. These are lending technologies that can be used to evaluate loan customers other than relationship lending which involves building personal relationships with the borrower over time.

capital, collateral and *conditions*—in assessing the chances of borrower default. Traditionally, relationship-driven banks rely on soft information collected on borrowers (through repeated interactions over time) as a basis for lending to informationally opaque SMEs. Thus, relationship lending and credit scoring techniques are the two main lending technologies predominantly used in small business lending. Nowadays, however, banks in developing credit markets are increasingly embracing other cutting edge techniques in assessing borrowers, such as psychometric scoring and judgmental score cards. This section examines in some detail the advantages and disadvantages of relationship lending and credit scoring techniques as well as gloss over other state of the art techniques now used in SME lending.

5.3.1 Relationship Lending

Under relationship lending, the acquisition of proprietary information over time about the entrepreneur, his line of business and the local business community is more important than formal financial ratios and other information readily available to the public. This is the essence of relationship banking, i.e. building proprietary information by developing relationships with customers over which will in turn be used to inform lending decisions.

5.3.1.1 Benefits of Relationship Lending

Boot (2000) enumerates a number of benefits of relationship banking: First, it improves information exchange between the lender and the borrower, thus *overcoming the problems of information asymmetry*. Thus, relationship lending allows banks to take better lending decisions (e.g. to accommodate good borrowers and screen out bad borrowers). In this regard therefore, relationships improve information quality and reduce the probability of discouragement for good borrowers in a competitive market. Second, it offers *flexibility and discretion in financial services contracting*. For example, under relationship lending, renegotiation of loan contract terms is relatively easier, unlike in capital markets where funding arrangements are rigid. Flexibility can also enhance investment efficiency (Schmeits 1999). In connection with flexibility, relationship lending can also accommodate *the intertemporal smoothing of contract terms*. For example, banks are often prepared to incur short-term bank losses for long-term gains when they offer subsidized credit to de novo corporations. Longer bank-borrower relationships have been found to reduce loan prices and the likelihood of the borrowing firm to pledge collateral (Petersen and Rajan 1994; Berger and Udell 1995).

A third benefit of relationship lending, according to Boot (2000), is that the use of loan covenants and other financial arrangements or contracts under relationship banking allows for *better control of potential conflicts of interest and reduces agency costs*. Fourth, the proximity between the bank and the borrower can *facilitate loan monitoring* especially in asset-based lending (e.g. in monitoring the value of collateral). This further enhances the acquisition of more proprietary information, which could potentially generate more lending for the borrower, and thus more rents for the bank. Relationship lending (based on multiple interactions with SME customers over time and/or across products) results in reduced screening and monitoring costs. In addition, because relationship lenders tend to have the advantage over non-relationship lenders in information processing and in monitoring of small business loans, it is thus expected that *loan quality[7] will be greater in relationship banks* than in non-relationship banks (Nakamura 1994). However, loan quality may not always be guaranteed even with information advantage and monitored lending, as there are other factors influencing loan quality including local economic conditions, geographical location of business, competition and other market factors (e.g. McNulty et al. 2001).

Fifth, due to their personal touch with customers, relationship lenders are arguably better able to offer a superior level of customer service than non-relationship lenders (Levonian and Soller 1996). Better services to customers could translate into additional business for the bank, which is often generated from customer satisfaction in previous or current lending relationships. In a study by Bharath et al. (2007), relationship lending has been found to generate *additional business for the relationship lender*. For example, a relationship lender may have a higher probability of selling information-sensitive products to its borrowers, which could potentially lead to the contracting of additional business, e.g. future lending business, debt/equity underwriting deals, and other fee based financial services. The results from Bharath et al. (2007) also show that the probability of a relationship lender providing a future loan is 42 %, while for a non-relationship lender, this probability is 3 % (Bharath et al. 2007). In essence, relationship lending by banks results in greater customer satisfaction derived from offering superior services to customers, which in turn produces repeat business for the bank.

Ultimately, for relationship lending to be considered an effective or valuable lending technique, it must enhance profitability and shareholder value. The primary concern here is whether relationship lenders are more profitable in SME lending than non-relationship lenders. While relationship lenders tend to make use of 'soft' information based on relationships and personal interactions in making non-standardised loans and offering customised financial services (e.g. De Young et al. 2004; Carter and McNulty 2005), the focus of non-relationship lenders is on the use of 'hard' information to make standardised loans and produce uniform types of financial services (e.g. credit card loans). Under these circumstances, relationship lenders and non-relationship lenders will have different ways of attaining high profits (Akhigbe and McNulty 2005). In some studies on the profitability of SME lending, Berney et al. (1998) found using a multivariate analysis that *relationship*

---

[7]Loan quality is measured in at least four ways: non-performing loans; loan loss provisions; net impairment charges (set off against loss reserves); and other real estate loans (all as a percentage of total loans).

lenders (referring to small banks) earn higher profit rates on SME loans than other assets on average. Even after controlling for various types of bank risk (credit, capital, funding, and liquidity risks), asset size and market competition, they still find that *SME loans contribute positively and significantly to bank profits.* In other words, the result displaces the common belief that small business loans are too risky to indulge and should be done away with. Also revealed from their study is the fact that relationship lenders have a higher tolerance for risk than other banks. Relationship lenders tend to be more aggressive in committing investible funds to small business loans than do non-relationship lenders.

From the above analysis, we can summarize the economic benefits of relationship lending *vis-à-vis* a range of outcomes:

(i) *Information Efficiency in Loan Origination*: the adequacy of information gathered is very useful in loan decision making, particularly in screening out low quality applications.
(ii) *Cost Effectiveness of Relationship Lendingi* Relationship lending reduces the unit cost of making a loan, i.e. (screening costs) as well as the cost of monitoring customers after the loan has been granted.
(iii) *Additional Business:* Relationship lending generates repeat business for the bank, as satisfied small business customers undertake additional financial services business. Moreover, a relationship lender's informational advantage over a non-relationship lender is likely to make the cross selling of financial services products more successful.
(iv) *Profitability*: Relationship lenders tend to be more profit efficient than non-relationship lenders, at least from a long-term perspective. Profitability is measured in several ways, one of which is the risk-adjusted returns on SME loans.

5.3.1.2 Costs of Relationship Lending

The benefits notwithstanding, relationship lending has been criticized on several grounds. First, it is widely held that because it is difficult and costly for financial intermediaries to obtain reliable information on SMEs, relationship lending is thus very costly. Because asymmetric information is relatively more associated with SMEs than large businesses, banks especially large ones have resorted to the use of impersonal approaches in lending to SMEs. Impersonal lending approaches refer mostly to those lending practices that support lending at a distance because of certain characteristics of the SME borrower or his firm. Such lending practices might involve more of the use of mail or telephone conversations rather than frequent personal visits to the bank as relationship banks do (see Berger et al. 2005).

Apart from the diseconomies of scale, a second pitfall of relationship lending is the fact that it *takes a long time to make loans* on the basis of relationship lending, since the bank must acquire as much information as possible to be able to extend loans to credit-worthy businesses. On the other hand, empirical evidence reveals that decisions on credit-scored loans (used mostly in advanced credit markets) tend to be taken relatively easier and faster than relationship-based loans and could be carried out over greater distances (e.g. Craig et al. 2005). Relationship banks are unable to effectively *penetrate new markets* without having to bear the cost of establishing branch networks. This assertion is corroborated by Anderson (2007) when he stated that '… relationship lending is appropriate in communities where lender and borrower had personal knowledge of each other, but is inefficient in an era of high customer mobility and extended branch networks' (p. 7).

Unlike relationship-based approaches, research has found that the use of credit scoring reduces the cost of information between borrowers and lenders (Frame et al. 2001:813) as well as the time and human input involved in reviewing loan applications (e.g. Feldman 1997). Because data has replaced experience, the role of underwriters and human judgement in credit decisions, as used in less developed credit markets, is now less important. To the extent that distance lending is now feasible, most non-relationship banks tend to keep an arm's length from their customers and tend to invest less in building relationships.

Boot (2000:16–17) also explains the 'dark sides' of relationship banking using two key phases. First is the 'soft budget constraint' problem and the second is the 'hold-up' problem. Soft budget constraint refers to the problems that banks face when it appears that they are 'tied in' in a relationship as the borrower's main source of external finance. There is therefore a tendency for borrowers to have perverse incentives to compel their banks to grant additional loans to forestall default on previously issued credit. The proximity that relationship banking affords may make banks to soften (rather than being tough on) their approach to the enforcement and/or renegotiation of loan contracts. One possible solution to this problem is to enforce collateral and grant seniority of debt claims to banks. This will facilitate timely intervention when a default is looming and insulate banks from undesirable consequences (Boot 2000). The hold-up problem occurs because the proprietary information that banks obtain of firms gives them information monopoly and market power, which may result in lending to firms at non-competitive rates in the future. This means that lenders may use long-term implicit contracts where they charge higher loan rates in the long term to compensate for subsidized rates granted to borrowers in the short term (Sharpe 1990; Rajan 1992). A firm's reaction to the hold-up problem may be to withdraw from borrowing from the bank, but this could lead to loss of potentially viable investment opportunities. Another solution could be to resort to multiple bank relationships. Again, this may prove to be costly because it is difficult for the firm's new bankers to get the primary lender to transfer soft information it has gathered on the firm over time. Moreover, it could even exacerbate the problem of credit availability (Ongena and Smith 2000). Another argument is that more competition could discourage relationships[8] (Berlin

---

[8]The nature of the contract terms between a bank and a firm, and hence the amount of profit that the bank retains over the life of the lending relationship depends on the number and behaviour of the bank's competitors, including both banks and non-bank lenders, e.g. finance companies (see details in Berlin 1996).

1996; Boot 2000) and undermine the value of information (Chan et al. 1986). Fierce inter-bank competition may reduce the ability and willingness of banks to fund de novo corporations. That is, competition may make credit subsidy to young firms unsustainable, and hence frustrate the intertemporal pricing of loans.

The following points summarize the economic costs or downsides of relationship lending:

(i)   *Cost Ineffectiveness*: Relationship lending consumes a lot of time and relies too much on human input to assess the credit worthiness of a borrower. Moreover, relationship banks are unable to issue standardized loans at relatively lower costs. Due to these setbacks, investing in relationships is not cost-effective.

(ii) *Inadequate Information*: In many cases, relationship lending does not seem to incorporate hard (quantitative) information on the borrower due to its relative absence for SMEs. It relies mainly on soft information gathered over time through relationship development.

(iii) *Adverse Selection*: Soft information on borrowers is hardly adequate and hence lending decisions taken based on inadequate or limited information could often be subjective and wrong. This tends to discourage risk-based pricing of loans and may eventually lead to inefficient credit rationing process.

(iv) *Undue Relaxation of Credit Terms*: Because relationship lending allows for flexibility in loan contracting, it could sometimes lead to undue relaxation of loan terms, especially when evaluating loans granted to longer-term bank customers. This is because of the implicit principal agent problem which 'relationships' between loan officers and borrowers sometimes entail, which could in effect limit the short-term profit maximisation objective of the relationship bank.

(v)   *Shift away from Traditional Lending to fee Income*: Because traditional SME lending is costly and risky, relationship banks could prefer to finance SMEs through other means (e.g. asset-based lending, leasing, etc.) and provide other financial management services to them.

5.3.2 Small Business Credit Scoring (SBCS)

With revolutions in technology, lending decisions are now made using the credit score of the small business owner. Many banks, especially large ones now rely significantly on credit scoring to assess the riskiness of less transparent SMEs. Credit scoring is an automated lending technique, which involves the use of historical data and statistical measures to ascertain or quantify the likelihood that a borrower will default on a loan. The history of credit scoring dates back to the 1950s when it was first used by American finance houses and credit card issuers to process credit applications. Although not an entirely new approach to consumer lending, the use of credit scoring for business lending was only introduced during the mid-1990s[9] (Akhavein et al. 2005; Berger and Frame 2005). Before now, credit scoring was mostly used in credit cards and mortgage lending for approving or rejecting credit card applications, for soliciting applications and for setting or adjusting terms on credit cards.

The rationale for adopting credit scoring is to enhance the efficiency of lending decisions by improving the predictive ability of loan applicants' chances of business success so that the lender is able to determine whom to accept (good borrowers) and whom to reject (bad borrowers). Credit scoring has also led to the profitability of small business lending by increasing the speed of underwriting. In fact, credit scoring has fundamentally changed the nature of loan underwriting altogether. Large banks are increasingly dominating the small business lending market by adopting automated and centralized systems in processing high-volume credit applications even in areas where they do not have extensive branch networks. They now make loans without any face-to-face contact or by relying on third party information. This development has particularly important implications for smaller banks that tend to rely hugely on relationship loans for their profitability and survival. In fact, there is a current debate that technological revolutions are beginning to give large banks an advantage over smaller banks through the use of credit scoring and other quantitative techniques, which automate lending decisions.

5.3.2.1   Advantages of Credit Scoring

Credit scoring makes it easier for large banks to make large pool of loans faster, cheaper and over great distances. Credit scoring has thus been viewed as an alternative technology to relationship lending technology. It tends to replace traditional lending technique based on subjective assessments of prospective borrowers—e.g. previous loan repayment performance, current capacity and willingness to repay, the presence of collateral and other forms of security and/or guarantees. These (subjective) assessments are predicated upon the loan underwriters' own experiences, taking into account not only historical information about the borrower but also considering the future prospects of the borrower (Anderson 2007). The emergence of credit scoring has enhanced objectivity in the loan approval process. This objectivity means that lenders are able to apply uniform underwriting criteria to borrowers irrespective of their gender, race, marital status or other factors that are deemed discriminatory under the Fed's *Equal Credit Opportunity Act* (see Mester 1997:8–9).

---

[9]As at 1995, only one bank, Wells Fargo Bank, had been able to generate a sufficiently large loan database to develop reliable proprietary model (Berger and Udell 2003). It has also be noted that Fair Isaac Corporation (FICO) was the first company to introduce its first Small Business Scoring System (SBSS) in 1995. Since then, many large banks have increasingly adopted SBCS as a technology for evaluating small business credit applicants (Berger and Frame 2005).

Developing an accurate method for evaluating small business loan applications can often prove difficult. This is because business loans differ substantially across borrowers and therefore requires sufficient historical data on loan performance and borrower characteristics to be able to build a reliable model that predicts corporate delinquencies and defaults. Credit scoring as a lending technology is mostly associated with large banks because they are able to build more reliable proprietary models from a large pool of loan database (Berger and Udell 2003:314). The implication of this is that while large banks enjoy potential economies of scale from dealing with high-volume loan applications, smaller banks do not have sufficient loan volume to develop their own proprietary models. Thus smaller banks still tend to utilize relationship lending because they believe that relationship provides them with a competitive advantage. Large banks are, however, able to adapt new technology and take advantage of scale economies to provide standardized services at relatively lower unit costs (Carter and McNulty 2005:1116).

The introduction of credit scoring may have significant effects on small business credit markets, including the availability, riskiness and pricing of loans as well as the interactions between the borrower and his lender. Numerous studies have found that the use of credit scoring is associated with an increase in small business lending, especially to relatively opaque small firms, risky borrowers, borrowers in low and moderate income areas, etc. (e.g. Frame et al. 2001, 2004; Berger and Frame 2005; Berger et al. 2005, 2009). On the efficiency of credit scoring models, research has found that the use of credit scoring reduces the cost of information between borrowers and lenders (Frame et al. 2001:813) as well as the time and human input involved in reviewing loan applications (Feldman 1997). Because data has replaced experience, the role of underwriters and human judgment in credit decisions is now less important. Although there is an argument in retail credit that it is implausible for underwriters to accurately interpret the signs, eventually, credit scores should have a high correlation with underwriters' assessments and a cost advantage for most consumer and small business lending (ibid.).

Changes in technology as exemplified by the use of credit scoring has also been found to enhance large banks' chances of making large amount of small business loans to small firms even in distant markets. This is because credit scoring makes the credit evaluation of loans faster and easier. Empirical evidence reveals that transactions-based loans tend to be carried out over greater distances and for longer periods of time than relationship-based loans (Craig et al. 2005). As credit scoring does not require a physical market presence, large banks can effectively penetrate new markets without having to bear the cost of establishing branch networks. This assertion is corroborated by Anderson (2007) when he stated "relationship lending is appropriate in communities where lender and borrower had personal knowledge of each other, but is inefficient in an era of high customer mobility and extended branch networks" (p. 7). For example, because of the use of scoring systems, borrowers in distant markets are able to obtain 'unsecure credit' from banks through 'direct marketing channels' (Akhavein et al. (2005:579). Thus, large banks because of their centralized structure are able to specialize in distance lending to small opaque businesses in order to beat their small bank competitors.

5.3.2.2 Pitfalls of Credit Scoring

In spite of its advantages, credit scoring as a lending technology is not without limitations. First, credit scoring has changed the relationship between borrowers and their lenders. Because large banks are able to extend credit to small businesses from a distance, they now keep an arm's length from their customers and tend to invest less in building relationships. A second disadvantage of credit scoring is that it lacks the forward-looking component, which is present in relationship lending since it only considers mostly previous information on the borrower. Thirdly, the accuracy of credit scoring models might be jeopardized if not based on balanced, reliable, and up-to-date information on both 'well-performing' and 'poorly performing' loans (Mester 1997:10). Fourth, large banks find it extremely difficult to monitor loans since a vast majority of their clients are outside their traditional lending market. Small banks tend not to have this constraint because they have a good knowledge of local market conditions in which most of their borrowers operate. Thus, smaller banks may be able to maintain their advantage over large banks in monitoring loans. For example, borrowers that fail to qualify for loans on the basis of credit scores or other forms of hard information but are nonetheless credit worthy on closer examination could possibly approach these relationship lenders as well (ibid., p. 13).

From the above analysis, we can summarize the main advantages and disadvantages of credit scoring below:

The main advantages of credit scoring are:

(i) *Quick, cost-effective loans*: it is easier for banks to make large pool of standardized loans faster, cheaper and over great distances. Credit scoring is cost-effective because it reduces the cost of information between borrowers and lenders as well as the time and human input involved in reviewing loan applications.

(ii) *Objectivity in loan decision-making*: The emergence of credit scoring enhances objectivity in the loan approval process, as lenders are able to apply uniform underwriting criteria to borrowers irrespective of their gender, race, marital status, or other discriminatory factors.

(iii) *Economies of Scale*: Large banks particularly enjoy economies of scale from dealing with high-volume loan applications. This is because they are able to build reliable proprietary models from a large pool of loan database.

The main pitfalls of credit scoring are:

(i) *Arm's length relationship*: Credit scoring has changed the relationship between borrowers and their lenders. Since large banks are able to extend credit to small businesses from a distance, they now keep an arm's length from their customers and tend to invest less in building relationships.

(ii) *Retrogressive*: Credit scoring lacks the forward looking component which is present in relationship lending since it only considers mostly previous information on the borrower.

(iii) *Model constantly needs revision*: The accuracy of credit scoring models might be jeopardized if not based on balanced, reliable, and up-to-date information on both 'well performing' and 'poorly performing' loans.
(iv) *Problem of monitoring distant loans*: Large banks find it difficult to monitor loans since a vast majority of their clients are outside their traditional lending market.

5.3.2.3 Credit Scoring Versus Relationship Lending: The Role of Organizational Structure

A few studies have revealed the important role of organizational structure in the use of credit scoring techniques. For example, Akhavein et al. (2005) show that banking organizations with fewer bank charters and more branch networks are more likely to adopt credit scoring technology and often do so rather quickly. This implies that large banks with a centralized structure are more likely to adopt SBCS. To the extent that credit scoring increases access to credit through distance lending which in turn reduces underwriting costs, it could result in lower cost of credit for some borrowers in the small business loan market. Empirical evidence suggests that credit scoring is associated with a larger allocation of large bank assets to small business lending, particularly to relatively risky "marginal applicants[10]" (Frame et al 2001; Berger et al. 2005).

But recent evidence tends to suggest that the use of SBCS does not appear to be peculiar to large banking organizations only. Even small banks have now embraced the technology. Using a unique survey data set obtained primarily for 330 community banks (with asset size less than $1 Billion) in US, Berger et al. (2009) found that the use of credit scoring in small business lending by community banks is surprisingly becoming widespread. However, most of the banks surveyed (about 86 %) appeared to use the credit scores of the small business owners (consumer credit scores, CCS) rather than the more robust scores (SBCS) that incorporate both the credit characteristics of the business firms and owners.

Nevertheless, the idea is that if small banks are beginning to increase their use of credit scoring, then the mainstream hypothesis that large banks tend to have an advantage in credit scoring still hangs in the balance. A case can be made for small banks that they might be able to catch up with large banks over time. In fact, there is an argument that small banks are able to learn from the mistakes of large banks especially with regards to previous costly write-offs from online banking experiments and other huge investments in technology, which did not yield superior results (e.g. Keeton 2000:46). Moreover, with their informational and relationship development advantages, small banks can still earn higher risk-adjusted returns on

---

[10]Marginal loan applicants refer to firms that satisfy at least one of the following conditions: (1) their owners have poor credit histories (2) they are five years or younger; (3) they have five or fewer employees (Jayaratne and Wolken 1999:445).

Table 5.1 Credit-scored lending versus relationship-based lending: summary of points

Credit-scored lending	Relationship-based lending
Based on hard (quantitative) information and impersonal relationships	Based on soft information gathered over time through relationship developments
Considers only historical information as a basis for predicting future performance of the borrowers	Considers both historical information and future prospects of the borrowers
Lending decisions are automated and objective. This tends to enhance risk-based pricing of loans and hence becomes a substitute for credit rationing (e.g. Feldman 1997)	Lending requires human input and subjective evaluation
Credit terms are less flexible with credit scoring and the lender rather tends to maximise profits period by period rather than over the life of a relationship (e.g. Mester 1997)	Allows for flexibility in loan contracting— e.g. inter-temporal smoothing of interest rates (see for example, Petersen and Rajan 1994; Berger and Udell 1995)
With advances in technology and the use of hard information, large banks are able to issue standardised loans (e.g. credit card loans) at relatively lower unit costs than small banks	Using soft information and relationship development, small banks tend to issue non-standardised loans, however, at relatively higher unit costs than large banks
Monitoring of borrowers is more expensive (most borrowers come from distant markets)	Monitoring is less expensive (most borrowers come from the local market)

loans (e.g. Carter et al. 2004) and can supplement relationship-based loans with credit scoring for more optimal performance of loans.[11] In fact, in the survey conducted by Cowan and Cowan (2006), respondents ranked relationship lending as more important than credit scores when making lending decisions irrespective of whether the bank used credit scoring or not. In other words, relationship lending still appears to be relevant and indeed a dominant factor in the lending decisions to small businesses. The practice by most banks regardless of size is to use credit scoring as a quantifiable measure of risk, which serves as a complement rather than a substitute for relationship banking.

The relative advantages/disadvantages of credit scoring and relationship-based lending can be summarized in Table 5.1.

5.3.3   Other Innovative Lending Techniques

As banks retrench in the wake of the global financial crisis, SMEs have found it increasingly hard to access finance they need to grow (Pierrakis and Collins 2013).

---

[11]A preview of the data collected by Berger et al. (2009) suggests that community banks that use credit scoring (though CSS) tend to have less loan performance problems than other banks, despite the observed increase in lending to more opaque borrowers.

Regardless of whether SMEs are simply less reliant on credit, or are merely tapping alternative sources of funding, the traditionally strong credit relationship between bank and business customer is eroding. Banks face the risk of being dis-intermediated in the emerging SME banking marketplace and pushed to the side as the unbundling of deposit, transaction and risk gathers momentum. According to Accenture (2011), there are four factors that drive the tipping point or unbundling of the SME market segment: (1) new regulation (pressure from government/regulators to lend to SMEs), (2) evolving customer needs (e.g. more money, innovative and tailored products with sound business advice), (3) the emergence of new players (enabled by technology), and (4) the erosion credit relationship (causing SMEs to use less credit or find alternative sources). In addition to the use of relationship lending and credit scoring techniques, banks, particularly in developing credit markets are increasingly embracing other cutting edge techniques, such as psychometric scoring and judgmental score cards, in assessing borrowers and offering them cost-effective financial services. Technological revolutions in advanced credit markets have also made electronic marketplaces possible, such as in peer-to-peer lending, where borrowers place request for loans online and private lenders bid to fund these loans. These new lending technologies are now reviewed below.

5.3.3.1 Use of Psychometrics

Psychometric scoring is a cutting-edge tool used to offer cost-effective non-collateral loans to SMEs. Psychometric tests are a computer-based questionnaire tool that assesses a borrower's personality traits and other traits known to differentiate between successful and unsuccessful entrepreneurs. These traits include factors like business aptitude, intelligence, innovation, locus of control, ethics, honesty, integrity, conscientiousness (dependability, industriousness, efficiency) and optimism, and so on (Anderson 2011). Certain other factors are often included as control variables, such as age, past business experience, and firm size (Acharya et al. 2007). They are currently being introduced to developing credit markets like India, Peru, Argentina, Mexico, South Africa, Kenya, Ghana, Nigeria, and Uganda who seem to have growing interest in making significant investments in data infrastructure and risk assessment models like advanced credit markets. They are used in micro-finance environments for improving access to low-cost financial services and enhancing financial inclusion. In some banks, SMEs are asked to provide a detailed business plan and repayment plan and then appraisal is done on the merits of the outcome of the psychometric test.

5.3.3.2 Judgmental Score Cards

In appraising SME loans, loan officers consider a wide range of factors such as financial capacity to repay loan, willingness to repay loan, collateral pledged, and the specific terms and conditions of the loan contract. At the same time, banks do not want credit analysts to spend hours spreading a small company's financial statements to underwrite a £5000 loan. The use of simple scorecard that evaluates a mix of financial and non-financial factors has been found to be the most appropriate way to appraise a large book of SME loans (Caire 2004). Banks that adopt this approach are able to make SME loan underwriting more cost-effective and are also be able to customize customer information to specific local economic and lender conditions. In developing credit markets where third-party information infrastructure is not fully developed, banks find it increasingly useful to mine their own institutional knowledge and historical portfolio data to develop scorecards that suit their strategies for the SME market segment. It is more sensible for banks in such markets to develop credit-scoring models that utilize judgmental scorecards to predict loan defaults.

Judgmental scorecards structure credit policies and management risk preferences into a mathematical model that ranks applicants according to risk. A judgmental model, unlike statistical models, can be created without any historical data, so it can be applied to new segments. The use of judgmental models can reduce the need to request collateral for loans granted to young and informationally opaque SMEs. The technique combines both financial and non-financial information about SMEs to make the default prediction models for SME loans more comprehensive and to have a higher chance of being more accurate than if only financial information was taken into consideration. Qualitative data relating to such variables as legal action by creditors to recover unpaid debts, company filing histories, comprehensive audit report/opinion data and firm-specific characteristics make a significant contribution to increasing the default prediction power of risk models built specifically for SMEs (see Altman et al. 2009).

5.3.3.3 Peer-to-Peer Lending

In the wake of the recent global financial crisis, there has been a rise of alternative finance intermediaries, particularly in the developed credit markets, due to SMEs' reduced access to credit from traditional banks. The evolution of information technology in recent years has led to the development of electronic marketplaces where commerce takes place remotely through the economic interaction of market participants. Within the financial services industry, a new and innovative method of loan origination has entered the credit market since 2005. This method of lending, known as 'peer-to-peer (P2P) lending', 'crowd funding' or 'social lending', is an online platform where borrowers place request for loans online and private lenders bid to fund these loans in an auction-like process (Klafft 2008). Online lending platforms are now available in a wide range of advanced countries, such as the US (Prosper Marketplace Inc., Lending Club Corporation), UK (Zopa Ltd, Funding Circle, Ratesetter, Wellesley, Assetz Capital), China (CreditEase, Lufax, Tuandai), Germany (Smava, Lendico, Zencap), and Japan (Maneo, Exchange Corporation KK) just to mention a few.

According to Baeck and Collins (2013), more than US$2.7 billion was raised through crowd funding globally in 2012, which helped to fund more than 1 million new projects. As of 30th June 2014, Lending Club dominated the US market for P2P lending, with a total of US$ 5.04 billion in issued loans, followed by its competitor, Prosper with US$ 1.6 billion. In the UK, Zopa Ltd dominates the market as the company has lent a total of £644 million worth of loans with more than 57,000 investors, while Funding Circle, the second largest platform has lent a total of £393.2 million at October 17, 2014 with 33,263 registered investors (see Table 5.2).

Overall, USA, China and UK have the largest share of the global peer-to-peer lending market. They make up 96 % of the overall financial return in the peer-to-peer lending market (Grant Thornton 2014). USA has the largest share, with about 51 %, while China and UK have 28 and 17 % respectively (see Fig. 5.1). In the UK alone, more than 5000 SMEs have raised funds through alternative finance intermediaries between 2011 and 2013.

There is an ongoing debate about disintermediation and the future relevance of traditional financial intermediaries fuelled by the increasing role of online lending platforms, where an electronic marketplace replaces a bank as the traditional intermediary and enables brokerage of consumer and business loans directly between borrowers and lenders (see Berger and Gleisner 2009). Thus, the growth in online P2P lending sector has important implications for competition for SME loans in traditional bank intermediaries. There is evidence to suggest that there is a difference in the lending model and competitive strategy of P2P lenders and their traditional bank counterparts. The main differentiation strategy between P2P lenders and traditional banks is the speed and ease of processing loan transactions due to the help of automated lending systems, which also help to reduce operating costs. In addition, investors in P2P lending markets also earn rates of return on their investment, which tend to be higher than those offered on traditional bank deposits (see Wang et al. 2009). The economic value created by P2P lending intermediaries for borrowers has been summarized by Pierrakis and Collins (2013) to include the following: (1) speed of securing finance, (2) competitive interest rates vis-à-vis traditional banks, (3) improved cash flow, (4) increase in employment, (5) business expansion and asset purchases, (6) increased overseas business growth, (7) increased sales, and (8) increased R&D activities, including new product development. The main economic benefits of P2P lending for lenders/investors are two fold: (1) higher average annualized returns on investment than traditional bank savings, and (2) possibility of risk diversification, evidenced by the ability to micromanage their investments.

5.4   Lending Infrastructure

The lending infrastructure is also a key element in determining the availability and quantum of credit supplied by banks to small businesses. The lending infrastructure refers to the rules and conditions provided mostly by governments or their regulatory agencies that affect financial institutions and their abilities to lend to different potential borrowers. According to Berger and Udell (2006), the lending

Table 5.2 Profile of major peer-to-peer lenders as at October 2014

Name of financial intermediary	Zopa Ltd.	Funding circle	Prosper marketplace Inc.	Lending club corporation
URL	www.zopa.co.uk	www.fundingcircle.co.uk	www.prosper.com	www.lendingclub.com
Year started Operation	2005	2010	2005	2007
Market	UK, Italy, Japan	US, UK	US	US
Lending sector (s)	Consumer lending only	Business lending only	Consumer lending only	Consumer and business lending
Lenders/investors	57,000	33,263	2 million+	n.a.
Borrowers	80,000+	5500 businesses	160,000	n.a.
Cooperating credit reporting agency	Equifax Inc.	n.a.	Experian Plc	TransUnion LLC
Loan processing bank	The Royal Bank of Scotland Plc	Santander UK	WebBank (Web-Financial Corp.)	WebBank (Web-Financial Corp.)
Regulator	FCA	FCA	State chartered	SEC
Maximum amount	£25,000	£1 million	US$35,000	US$100,000 (for business loans) US$35,000 (for personal loans)
Loan grades	n.a.	A+ to C−	AA-HR	A-G
Pricing of loans	4.8–6.9 % (by tenor)	6–15 % (by risk bands)	6.73–35.36 % APR	5.9–29.9 % (by credit grade)
Loan origination fees	n.a.	2–5 % (depending on tenor and type of credit)	1–5 % (depending on tenor)	1.11–5 %
Loan tenor	1–5 years	6 months–5 years	3–5 years	1–5 years
Average annual returns to investors	5.2 % for loans up to 5 years	6.4 % (after fees and bad debts, but before tax)	10.8 % net spread	5 % (A Grade); 7.3 % (B Grade); 8.67 % (C Grade)
Secondary market	Available (Italy only)	Available	Planned	Available
Total lending Volume to date	£644 million	£393.2 million	US$1.6 billion	US$5.04 billion

Sources P2P Intermediaries' website; Berger and Gleisner (2009)
n.a. not available

Fig. 5.1 Market share of the global peer-to-peer lending market (2013). *Source* Grant Thornton (2014)

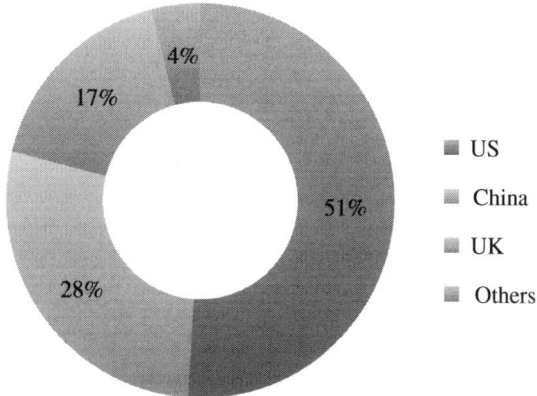

infrastructure consists of three environments: (a) the information environment (b) the legal, judicial and bankruptcy environment (c) the tax and regulatory environments. All of these elements may directly affect small business credit availability by affecting the extent to which the different lending technologies can be legally and profitably employed.

5.4.1 The Economics of Information

One important aspect of the information infrastructure is the accounting environment. As findings from the literature have revealed, SMEs do not keep adequate accounting records and as such are unable to satisfy the requirements of banks who rely very much on financial (hard) information in making informed lending decisions. A robust accounting standards and the use of credible independent accounting firms are necessary conditions for informative financial statements. These are also necessary conditions for the feasibility of many components of loan contracting. For example, financial covenants are not feasible if the financial ratios calculated from bank financial statements are not reliable (Berger and Udell 2006). Another important aspect of the information infrastructure is the availability of information on payment performance. Third party information exchanges or business credit bureaus provide a formal organizational mechanism for the exchange of commercial information on payment performance. The availability of commercial information like this has been shown to have power in predicting firm failure beyond financial ratios and other descriptive information about the firm (Kallberg and Udell 2003). Survey data in the US also indicates that without credit bureaus, the time to process loans, the cost of making loans, and the level of defaults would all be higher (Miller 2003).

5.4.2 The Legal, Judicial and Bankruptcy Environment

A country's legal and judicial infrastructure significantly influences the context in which loan contracting is conducted. The legal infrastructure that affects business lending consists of the commercial laws that specify the property rights associated with a commercial transaction and enforcement of these laws (Berger and Udell 2006). The latter determines the confidence of contracting parties in financial contracts. Collectively, these two features constitute the rule of law as it relates to the extension of credit. Banks cannot effectively deploy specific contracting elements (such as covenants, maturity, collateral and personal guarantees) without robust commercial and financial laws. According to Fleisig (1996), a number of legal reforms need to be implemented in order to develop the use of contracting elements like collateral (including movable assets) to secure loans, particularly in developing countries. These include: (1) changing the law to permit a greater variety of security interests in a wider range of transactions by a broader group of people; (2) making registry records public, reforming state-operated registries, restructuring public registries to permit competition, and privatizing registry services or allowing private registry services to compete with public ones; (3) speeding up enforcement and making it cheaper, changing the law to permit private parties to contract for non-judicial repossession and sale, and, when possible, allowing private parties to contract for repossession and sale without government intervention. The efficiency of bankruptcy system is also critical. How long a company stays in bankruptcy either in liquidation or in reorganization is important. Also important is the degree to which bankruptcy laws and their enforcement adhere to absolute priority. For example, the power of collateral will ultimately depend on whether the priority rights of secured lenders are upheld in bankruptcy.

5.4.3 The Tax and Regulatory Environment

The tax and regulatory environments may have direct effects on SME credit availability. A country's tax laws can either lure SMEs into the formal sector of the economy or keep them out of it. The tax system can inadvertently place SMEs at a disadvantage. For example, the taxation of manufacturers, traders and importers (e.g. import duty, sales tax, excise taxes, etc.) can affect the costs of doing business and profitability of businesses depending on the rate of taxation and hence either encourage or discourage bank lending to SMEs. The second element, the regulatory environment, may also restrict SMEs credit availability indirectly by constraining the potential financial institution structure. In this connection therefore, the enforcement of capital requirements and direct government intervention have the ability to directly influence the quantity and cost of lending to SMEs. There is a direct link between activities of bank regulators and bank lending behaviour, especially with respect to the enforcement of capital requirements. Banks generally have a number of options when improving its capital position. They can shrink assets by selling securities, selling other assets, charging off loans or reducing new lending. In many cases, the enforcement of capital-to-asset ratios leads to the shrinkage of new bank lending to bank-dependent customers (e.g. Peek and Rosengren 1995b). Governments also often intervene in the lending market to influence loan supply, e.g. through the use of *interest rate subsidies, directed lending to specific sectors, loan guarantee schemes,* and a variety of other approaches to get SMEs financed. However, the gap between SMEs and larger businesses remains. With the recent financial crisis, many economies are looking to SMEs to provide much needed jobs and to help pull their economies out of recession, putting SMEs back into the spotlight of development and political agendas.

References

Accenture (2011) Next generation SME banking: how banks can apply innovation to seize the SME revenue growth opportunity. http://www.accenture.com/SiteCollectionDocuments/gb-en/Accenture-Next-Generation-SME-Banking.pdf

Acharya V, Rajan A, Schoar A (2007) What determines entrepreneurial success? A psychometric study of rural entrepreneurs of India

Akhavein J, Frame WS, White LJ (2005) The diffusion of financial innovations: an examination of the adoption of small business credit scoring by large banking organizations. J Bus 78 (2):577–596

Akhigbe A, McNulty J (2005) Profit efficiency sources and differences among small and large U.S Commercial Banks. J Econ Financ 29(3) (Fall 2005)

Altman EI, Sabato G, Wilson N (2009) The value of non-financial information in SME risk management. Paper presented at the credit scoring and control XI conference, Edinburgh, Scotland, 26–28 Aug 2009

Anderson R (2007) The credit scoring toolkit: theory and practice for retail credit risk management and decision automation. Oxford University Press, UK, 792 pp

Anderson R (2011) Psychometrics: a new tool for small business lending. Practitioner paper presented at the credit scoring and control XII conference, Edinburgh, Scotland, 24–26 Aug

Avery RB, Samolyk KA (2004) Bank consolidation and the provision of banking services: small commercial loans. J Financ Serv Res 25:291–325

Baeck P, Collins L (2013) Working the crowd: a short guide to crowd funding and how it can work for you. Nesta 21 May 13

Beck T, Demirguc-Kunt A, Martinez Peria M (2008) Bank financing for SMEs around the world: drivers, obstacles, business models, and lending practices. World Bank Policy Research Working Paper 4785; Washington DC

Beck T, Demirguc-Kunt A, Martinez Peria M (2011) Bank financing for SMEs: evidence across countries and bank ownership types. J Financ Serv Res 39:35–54

Berger A, Frame WS (2005) Small business credit scoring and credit availability. Federal Reserve Bank of Atlanta, Atlanta

Berger SC, Gleisner F (2009) Emergence of financial intermediaries in electronic markets: the case of online P2P lending. Bus Res 2(1):39–65

Berger AN, Udell GF (1995) Relationship lending and lines of credit in small firm finance. J Bus 68:351–382

Berger AN, Udell GF (2003) Small business and debt finance. In: Acs ZJ, Audretsch DB (eds), Handbook of entrepreneurship research. Kluver Academic Publishers, Great Britain, pp 299–328

Berger AN, Udell GF (2006) A more complete conceptual framework for financing of small and medium enterprises. J Financ Bank 30(11):2945–2966

Berger AN, Saunders A, Scalise JM, Udell GF (1998) The effects of bank mergers and acquisitions on small business lending. J Financ Econ 50:187–229

Berger AN, Miller NH, Petersen MA, Rajan RG, Stein JC (2005a) Does function follow organisational form? Evidence from the lending practices of large and small banks. J Financ Econ 76:237–269

Berger A, Frame WS, Miller NH (2005b) Credit scoring and the availability, price and risk of small business credit. J Money Credit Bank 37:191–222

Berger AN, Rosen RJ, Udell GF (2007) Does market size structure affect competition? The case of small business lending. J Bank Financ 31: 11–33 (Elsevier)

Berger A, Cowan AM, Frame WS (2009) The surprising use of credit scoring in small business lending by community banks and the attendant effects on credit availability and risk. Working paper series, Federal Reserve Bank of Atlanta, Atlanta (2009-9)

Berlin M (1996) For better and for worse: three lending relationships. Bus Rev Fed Reserve Bank Phila 11:3–12

Bernanke BS, Lown CS (1991) The credit crunch. Brook Pap Econ Act 2:205–247

Berney R, Kolari J, Ou C (1998) The profitability of small business lending by small banks. SBA Off Advocacy, Small Bus Res Summ 184

Bharath S, Dahiya S, Saunders A, Srinivasan A (2007) So what do I get? The bank's view of lending relationships. J Financ Econ 85:368–419

Boot AWA (2000) Relationship banking: what do we know? J Financ Intermed 9:7–25

British Bankers Association (2011) Small business lending bank facts. Published 10 Oct 2011. http://www.bba.org.uk/media/article/small-business-lending-bankfacts/press-pack/. Accessed 20 Apr 2013

Caire D (2004) Building credit scorecards for small business lending in developing markets. Bannock Consulting, November

Carbo-Valverde S, Rodriguez-Fernandez F, Udell GF (2009) Bank market power and SME financing constraints. Rev Financ 13:309–340

Carter DA, McNulty JE (2005) Deregulation, technological change, and the business-lending performance of large and small banks. J Bank Financ 29:1113–1130

Carter DA, McNulty JE, Verbrugge JA (2004) Do small banks have an advantage in lending? An examination of risk-adjusted yields on business loans at large and small banks. J Financ Serv Res 25:233–252

Cavallo L, Rossi PS (2001) Scale and scope economies in the European banking systems. J Multinatl Financ Manage 11:515–531

Chan YS, Greenbaum SI, Thakor AV (1986) Information reusability, competition and bank asset quality. J Bank Financ 10:255–276

Cole RA, Goldberg LG, White LJ (2004) Cookie-cutter versus character: the micro structure of small business lending by large and small banks. J Financ Quant Anal 39(2):227–251

Coppola F (2014) The money multiplier is dead. Pieria, 13 Mar 2014. Available at http://www.pieria.co.uk/articles/the_money_multiplier_is_dead. Accessed 30 Dec 2014

Cowan CD, Cowan AM (2006). A survey based assessment of financial institution use of credit scoring for small business lending. SBA Office of Advocacy, November, 62 pp

Craig BR, Jackson WE III, Thomson JB (2005) The role of relationships in small-business lending. Fed Reserve Bank Clevel Econ Comment ISSN 0428-1276 (15 Oct)

De la Torre A, Martinez Peria M, Schmukler SL (2010) Bank involvement with SMEs: beyond relationship lending. J Bank Financ 34:2280–2293

DeYoung R, Hunter WC, Udell GF (2004) The past, present, and probable future for community banks. J Financ Serv Res 25(2/3):85–133

Duan H, Han X, Yang H (2009) An analysis of causes for SMEs financing difficulty. Int J Bus Manag 4(6):73–75

Erel I (2006) The effect of bank mergers in loan prices: evidence from the US. The Ohio State University, US

Feldman R (1997) Banks and a big change in technology called credit scoring. Reg Fed Reserve Bank Minneap 19–25

Fleisig H (1996) Secured transactions: the power of collateral. Financ Dev 44–46

Frame WS, Srinivasan A, Woosley L (2001) The effect of credit scoring on small business lending. J Money Credit Bank 33:813–825

Frame WS, Padhi M, Woolsey L (2004) Credit scoring and the availability of small business credit in low-and moderate income areas. Financ Rev 39:34–54

Gilbert RA (2000a) Nationwide branch banking and the presence of large banks in rural areas. Fed Reserve Bank of St Louis Rev 82:13–28

Gilbert RA (2000b) Big fish, small ponds: large banks in rural communities. Reg Econ (July 2000)

Hubbard G, Kuttner K, Palia D (2002) Are there bank effects in borrowers' costs of funds? Evidence from a matched sample of borrowers and banks. J Bus 75(4):559–581

Jayaratne J, Wolken JD (1999) How important are small banks to small business lending? New evidence from a survey of small firms. J Bank Financ 23:427–458

Kallberg JG, Udell GF (2003) Private information exchange in the United States. In: Miller MJ (ed) Credit reporting systems and the international economy. MIT Press, Cambridge, pp 203–227

Keeton WR (1995) Multi-office bank lending to small businesses: some new evidence. Fed Reserve Bank Kansas City Econ Rev 81:63–75

Keeton WR (2000) The transformation of banking and its impact on customers and small businesses. Econ Rev First Q Fed Reserve Bank Kansas City 86(1):25–53

Klafft M (2008) Online peer-to-peer lending: a lenders' perspective. Available at http://papers.ssrn.com/sol3/papers.cfm?abstract_id=1352352. Accessed 17 Oct 2014

Levonian ME, Soller J (1996) Small banks, small loans, small business. Weekly Letter, Federal Reserve Bank of San Francisco

McNulty JE, Akhigbe AO, Verbrugge JA (2001) Small bank loan quality in a deregulated environment: the information advantage hypothesis. J Econ Bus 53:325–339

Mester LJ (1997) What's the point of credit scoring? Bus Rev Fed Reserve Bank Phila 3:3–16

Miller MJ (2003) Credit reporting systems and the international economy. MIT Press, Cambridge, 465 pp

Nakamura LI (1994) Small borrowers and the survival of the small bank: is mouse bank mighty or mickey? Fed Reserve Bank Phila Bus Rev 3–15 (Nov/Dec)

Ogura Y, Uchida H (2007) Bank consolidation and soft information acquisition in small business lending. RIETI Discussion paper series 07-E-037

Ongena S, Smith DC (2000) What determines the number of bank relationships? Cross-country evidence. J Financ Intermed 9:26–56

Peek J, Rosengren S (1995a) Small business credit availability: how important is the size of lender? In: Working papers 95-5. Federal Reserve Bank of Boston, Boston

Peek J, Rosengren E (1995b) Bank regulation and the credit crunch. J Bank Financ 19:679–692

Petersen MA, Rajan RG (1994) The benefits of firm-creditor relationships: evidence from small business data. J Financ 49:3–37

Pierrakis Y, Collins L (2013) Banking on each other: the rise of peer-to-peer lending to businesses. Nesta 25(04):13

Rajan RG (1992) Insiders and outsiders: the choice between informed and arm's-length debt. J Financ 47:1367–1400

Rauch JH, Hendrickson JM (2004) Does consolidation hurt the small business borrower? Small Bus Econ 23:219–226

Schmeits A (1999) Discretion in bank contracts and the firm's funding source choice between bank and financial market financing. Working Paper, Washington University

Schmieder C, Marsch K, Aerssen K (2010) Does banking consolidation worsen firms' access to credit? Evidence from the German economy. Small Bus Econ 35:449–465

Sharpe SA (1990) Asymmetric information, bank lending, and implicit contracts: a stylized model of customer relationships. J Financ 45:1069–1087

Stein JC (2002) Information production and capital allocation: decentralised versus hierarchical firms. J Financ 57:1891–1921

Strahan PE, Weston JP (1998) Small business lending and the changing structure of the banking industry. J Bank Financ 22:821–845

Thornton G (2014) Alternative lending: a regulatory approach to peer-to-peer lending. Available at http://www.grant-thornton.co.uk/Documents/financial-services/Alternative-Lending-regulatory-approach-to-Peer-to-Peer-lending.pdf. Accessed 17 Oct 2014

Venkatesh J, Kumari RL (2011) Issues and perspectives of financing SME sector. Int J Financ Manage Res Dev 1(1):11–21

Wang H, Greiner M, Aronson JE (2009) People-to-people lending: the emerging e-commerce transformation of a financial market. In: ML Nelson et al (ed) Value creation in e-business management, vol 36. LNBIP, pp 182–195

Williamson O (1967) The economics of defense contracting: incentives and performance in issues. In: McKean R (ed) Defense economics. Columbia University Press, New York

Williamson O (1988) Corporate finance and corporate governance. J Financ 43:567–591

Zavatta R (2008) Financing technology entrepreneurs and SMEs in developing countries. Info Dev/World Bank, Washington, DC

Part IV
Determinants of Loan Contract Terms

Abstract This part incorporates major theoretical works on loan pricing, collateral determination and the value of relationships in loan contracting. Findings from this part reveal that the determinants of risk premium on SME loans are largely connected with factors that underline the opacity and riskiness of SMEs and are also connected with lender factors such as cost of funds and administrative expenses associated with loan appraisal and disbursement. Banks generally charge higher differential interest rates to younger SMEs than to older, larger and more established customers, due to the former's relative opacity, perceived risks and uncertainties and high failure rate. Customers with longer relationships with their bank tend to benefit from lower interest rates than first-time customers, supporting the notion that relationship lending generates valuable information about borrower quality. What determines the likelihood of requesting collateral from SMEs is significantly related to the borrower's risk characteristics, such as firm size, firm's age or opacity. Loan size, firm size and borrower's credit rating tend to also determine the likelihood that a bank will request full or partial collateralisation. Finally, the determinants of loan contract terms are also influenced by external and business environment factors such as the business cycle, monetary policy and the level of bank competition.

Keywords Loan contract terms · SMEs · Risk premium · Collateral · Borrower factors · Lender factors · Business environment

Chapter 6
Determinants of SME Loan Contracts

6.1 Determinants of Risk Premium on SME Loans

As reviewed earlier in part 2, there are two competing theories that explain the riskiness of SME lending. While the information asymmetry model championed by Stiglitz and Weiss (1981) explains the riskiness of SMEs from the perspective of their relative opacity and informational deficiencies, the main thrust of Post-Keynesian credit rationing theory relates to the idea of "fundamental uncertainty", which characterizes the outcome of most investment projects (Wolfson 1996) and hence determines the risk premium of such projects. This section examines the micro-level determinants of the risk premium on SME loans. It also examines the external factors influencing loan profitability. A large amount of studies have identified the relationship between loan pricing and a number of borrower, loan and relationship characteristics (e.g. Petersen and Rajan 1994; Berger and Udell 1995; Harhoff and Korting 1998; Lehmann and Neuberger 2001, etc.). We now examine in some detail the influence of these factors on risk pricing of SME loans.

6.1.1 Borrowing Firm's Characteristics and Risk Premium

6.1.1.1 Firm Size

Banks are likely to charge higher differential interest rates to SMEs than to large customers. It is generally believed that smaller firms are more prone to insolvency than large firms because they are usually less diversified on the production and distributions side and are more likely to face financing constraints (Behr and Guttler 2007). This notion is taken into consideration by banks that do not grant credit to high-risk default risk borrowers. In an empirical study of German SMEs, Harhoff

© The Author(s) 2016
V.U. Ekpu, *Determinants of Bank Involvement with SMEs*,
SpringerBriefs in Finance, DOI 10.1007/978-3-319-25837-9_6

and Korting (1998) observed a negative relationship between firm size and interest rates, indicating that banks may use firm size as a proxy for credit risk. Lehmann and Neuberger (2001) and D'Auria et al. (1999) obtained similar results for Italy and Germany. The reputational effects and greater negotiating power associated with larger firms could help in explaining why they obtain longer-term loans, pay lower interest rates and provide less collateral than their smaller counterparts.

6.1.1.2   Firm's Age/Opacity

Conventional wisdom in contemporary corporate finance literature argues that younger SMEs are more likely to be less transparent or informationally opaque. Hyytinen and Pajarinen (2008) find that a closely related proxy for informational opacity is a firm's age. Informationally opaque firms are likely to have poor financial records. As noted earlier, it is expected that a firm that has good financial records will be able to convince a bank of its ability to repay a loan. The absence of formal financial records thus increases the credit risk of a firm. In the context of Sub-Saharan Africa, Lefilleur (2009) advanced a number of reasons for the acute information asymmetry between young SMEs and their bankers: First, most SMEs evolve in the informal sector and are therefore not in a position to give banks the minimum information they generally require (e.g. contact details, legal documents, financial statements, etc.). In addition, for SMEs evolving in the formal sector, the excessively high level of accounting information required by international/regional financial reporting standards, coupled with the lack of independent, competent and credible accounting firms, have an impact on the quality of information transmitted to banks. Moreover, some entrepreneurs knowingly disseminate very limited or even erroneous information in order to evade taxes. Finally, there are usually no tools that would allow banks to learn about the payment behaviors of their new clients. Credit referencing agencies either do not exist or are ineffective. In this context, banks use informal communication to make up for the shortfall in financial information.

Given this background, banks are therefore likely to charge higher interest rates to younger and informationally opaque SMEs and lower rates to older and more established large firms. Stiglitz and Weiss's (1981) model show that with a given creditworthiness, relatively young firms seeking external finance are likely to be more credit constrained than a pool of more established firms. Diamond (1989) also shows that the joint influence of adverse selection and moral hazard reduces the ability of a recent entrant to raise external finance at a reasonable cost. These problems are most severe when the firm is young (i.e. a start-up) and has only a short track record, because then a severe enough adverse selection (leading to high interest rates) undermines the firm's incentives to behave diligently (e.g. to choose a low risk investment project) as shown by Stiglitz and Weiss (1981). If the firm survives to the next period despite its risky investment decision, adverse selection is less of a problem, for those that survive are, on the average, of better quality. This decreases the interest rates that the financiers demand and thus increases the firm's incentive to choose less risky projects over time.

6.1.1.3 Availability of Collateral/Guarantees

Generally speaking, banks are likely to charge higher interest rates for SME loan applicants that cannot meet the bank's collateral requirements. On a theoretical basis, the use and strength of personal or business collateral supplied by the borrower should decrease the lender's risk and hence, improve financing conditions (Bruns and Fletcher 2008; St-Pierre and Bahri 2011). The bank may insist on a personal commitment from the owner-manager in addition to company guarantees, ensuring alignment of interests between bank and borrower and reducing monitoring costs for the bank (Jimenez and Saurina 2004). Under these circumstances, the availability of collateral and/or guarantee should reduce interest rates. Secured loans tend to carry lower loss given default and will lead to lower risk premiums. This is the "loss mitigation" effect (Berger et al. 2011). However, some studies have also found that the use of collateral is a signal of high probability of default and is not associated with reduced risk premium (see St-Pierre and Bahri 2011). This reflects the argument that banks use collateral to control presumed risk, because young, small, more indebted and less solvent firms are more likely to be asked to guarantee loans. The finding suggests that the dominant reason collateral banks require collateral is to help detect riskier borrowers ("lender selection" effect).

6.1.1.4 Firm/Owner's Credit Rating

The interest rate a bank charges its business customers is likely to be a decreasing function of the applicant firm's/owner's credit rating. Credit risk is related to the firm's financial standing and its ability to meet its financial obligations. According to Bruns and Fletcher (2008), the lender's probability of advancing credit to the borrower could be dependent on both past performance and current financial standing of the borrower. Past performance, measured by profit and losses in the past increases or decreases the financial strength of the firm. In addition, the number of business credit obligations on which the firm has been delinquent in the past is a negative function of the quantity and cost of credit extended to the firm. Current financial position is mainly an indicator of whether or not the borrower is solid enough to repay the loan should the individual project that money is sought for fail. Therefore, the effect of financial standing on the credit decision is similar to that of collateral—a strong financial position indicates that the borrower is able to repay the loan irrespective of the outcome of the project. Machauer and Weber (1998) confirm in their study a highly significant impact of credit rating on loan prices, with a better rating lowering the cost of capital.

6.1.2   Lender Characteristics and Risk Premium

The pricing of loans to businesses can more closely be explained in terms of the *cost, revenue* and *risk* elements associated with lending activity. As we know, the profitability of any venture is directly determined by two major components: cost and revenue. The revenue components of lending include interest income and other non-interest fees. *Interest income* is interest earned on loans and other earning assets. The importance of interest income to profitability is dependent on the relative proportion of earning assets (compared to non-earning assets) in a bank's total asset portfolio (Gup and Walter 1989). Apart from interest income, banks also earn revenue from fees charged on loans (Churchill and Lewis 1986) and similar financial services such as hire purchase, factoring and other asset-based lending.

The BBA (2011) has identified three key drivers behind how banks price lending to SMEs: (1) cost of funds, (2) cost of risk and capital, and (3) cost of administration. The literature shows that banks are likely to charge higher risk premiums on SME loans because of higher cost of funds, cost of risk and costs of loan administration.

6.1.2.1   Cost of Funds

The risk premium on loans is usually affected by the cost of mobilizing liquidity and accessing capital. According to the loanable funds theory, in order to lend money to businesses, banks need to attract funds from depositors by paying them interest. They also need to aim to hold deposits for similar lengths of time as the term of loans financed. Hubbard et al. (2002) in a recent study investigated the effects of banks' financial condition on the borrowers' risk premium after controlling for borrower risk and information costs. They find that capital-constrained banks charge higher loan rates than well-capitalised banks and that this cost difference is especially associated with borrowers for which 'information costs' and 'incentive problems' are most important (pp. 561). Their result is also consistent with models that allow banks to charge a risk premium to borrowers facing switching costs in bank-borrower relationships as well as models of the bank-lending channel of monetary transmission. The former concept refers to borrowers that switch from one bank to the other in search of better credit relationships and have to bear the costs of building credit reputation and transferring proprietary information to the new lender. The latter concept is explained below under the credit channel of monetary policy.

6.1.2.2   Cost of Risk and Cost of Holding Capital

Costs can also be reckoned in terms of the risks associated with bank lending such as funding liquidity, credit, and capital risks. All banks face the risk of maturity transformation of assets and liabilities. They borrow short-term funds (liquid liabilities) to finance long-term (illiquid) loans so that there is a disconnection between their short term funding and their expected future cash flows. Banks are therefore exposed to 'funding liquidity risk' (Brunnermeier et al. 2009) and this affects their profitability and long-run survival. For example, if banks face unexpected withdrawal of deposits on a large scale and are unable to control the resulting cash shortage by borrowing from money markets, they may be forced into early liquidation of their assets (i.e. fire sale) in order to realise cash, thus lowering their book value. The situation becomes worse if contagion occurs: the entire banking system will become vulnerable to destructive bank runs (Diamond and Dyvbig 1983) and confidence in the system will disappear quickly as the entire credit markets cease to function.

Banks also face credit risk or the risk that a borrower or counterparty will be unable to repay a loan or interest due on the loan on the due date. Mainstream theory suggests that increased exposure to credit risk is normally associated with lower bank profitability (e.g. Athanasoglou et al. 2008). However, in Post-Keynesian economics, banks are equally prepared to face higher credit risk with large firms because lending to them is more profitable, while small borrowers are likely to have a higher possibility of deviation from their expected rate of return than large firms due to uncertainty and other factors such as competition and macroeconomic conditions (Basu 2003). In any case, banks are able to improve credit risk through effective screening and monitoring of borrowers. There is some evidence that large bank institutions are less likely to lend to relatively young and informationally opaque entities because they lack good credit reputation and hence could pose serious credit risks to lenders (Haynes et al. 1999; Berger and Udell 2006). On the liability side, banks could be significantly dependent on a particular source of funding, e.g. borrowing heavily from the wholesale interbank markets or through securitisations.

Now turning to capital risk, banks are highly levered financial institutions and the volume of their businesses is in multiples of their regulatory capital. According to the Basel capital accord, banks are required to keep about 8 % of their assets in capital (CAR). Banks are required to hold adequate capital to cushion the risks of loan losses and insulate depositors by providing a first line of reserve to absorb such losses. However, increased nominal capital requirements often results in banks taking on extra risks on their portfolios, and this could, under some circumstances, actually increase the probability of bank failure, even if it improves the bank's franchise value.[1]

6.1.2.3 Administration Costs

Administration costs refer to the costs directly associated with the loan administration and monitoring function, e.g. salaries of loan officers and other support staff,

---

[1]Franchise value means the present value of the bank's stream of future profits.

benefits and other loan-related office expenses such as telephone bills, postage, photocopying, transportation, etc. (Churchill and Lewis 1986: 197). Smaller loan facilities tend to have a relatively higher administrative cost per unit of currency lent than larger facilities, and not all of that cost can be recovered through fees. So small loans tend to bear higher margins, even if the risk is comparable with larger lending. Because of their size, large banks are likely to incur higher operating and monitoring costs for smaller loans than for larger loans due to diseconomies of scale. This suggests that most large banks are likely to lend predominantly to larger corporates that seek out larger loans, and hence find relationship lending to small local customers less cost effective and profitable.

6.1.3   The Role of Relationships in Loan Pricing

As examined in Sect. 5.3.1, relationship lending involves the acquisition of soft information by the lender about the prospective borrower through one-to-one personal contact over time in which case the loan officer uses the soft information obtained to make lending decisions. The length of borrower-lender relationships can influence the setting of loan contract terms. Boot and Thakor (1994) show that when lenders and borrowers engage in repeated interactions through time, they are able to build trust and credibility, which help to reduce moral hazard problems. Banks that have gathered proprietary information over their clients often use this information in refining contract terms offered to borrowers. Berger and Udell (1995) in their study of the role of relationships in determining both price and non-price contract terms of bank lines of credit extended to firms find that longer bank- borrower relationships reduce the interest rates paid by borrowers and the chances that they will have to pledge collateral.[2] To the extent that this occurs, longer duration of banking relationships relaxes the terms of a loan, ameliorates credit constraints and hence raises firm value. Several studies have also found that relationship driven banks are able to benefit from the inter-temporal smoothing of contract terms—e.g. by sacrificing short-term for long-term gains when they offer subsidized credit to growing enterprises (Sharpe 1990; Rajan 1992; Petersen and Rajan 1994, 1995; Berger and Udell 1995; Berlin and Mester 1998; Boot 2000). In other words, banks are likely to charge younger firms lower interest rates at the beginning of their banking relationship with the hope of making higher returns in later years when their business has become established. All these results are

---

[2]According to Boot et al. (1991), collateral is an alternative to trust and by developing relationships, it is expected that collateral requirements would be more relaxed. Jimenez and Saurina (2004) also found that the likelihood of collateral is lower in more concentrated credit markets and for loans made to borrowers with longer relationship with the lender that grants the loan.

consistent with theoretical arguments that relationship lending generates valuable information about borrower quality.

Since relationship lending involves a personal touch with local customers, relationship-driven banks by virtue of their proximity to the local customers are arguably more efficient than their non-relationship banks in delegated monitoring and enforcement of loan contracts (Diamond 1984; Nakamura 1994). This in turn improves loan quality, though this may not necessarily improve lending profitability because small loans are also associated with higher costs of lending as literature suggests. In addition, through multiple interactions with the customer, smaller banks are able to appraise their clients' investments and provide support services (e.g. business planning, accounting and tax planning solutions etc.) in order to add real value to the client and ensure better cash flow.

6.1.4   External Factors Affecting SME Loan Pricing

Apart from borrower and lender factors, a number of external factors impact on the pricing of SME loans. These include the credit channel of monetary policy, the credit market structure and business cycle fluctuations, among other external or macroeconomic factors.

6.1.4.1   The Credit Channel of Monetary Policy

According to the credit channel theory presented by Bernanke and Gertler (1995), the direct effects of monetary policy actions such as changes in short term interest rates are amplified by endogenous changes in the external finance premium (EFP), where EFP = cost of funds raised externally (by issuing equity and debt) and cost of funds raised internally (by retaining earnings/profits). The size of the EFP reflects imperfections in the credit markets that drive a wedge between the expected return received by lenders and the costs faced by potential borrowers. Accordingly, a change in monetary policy (i.e. an increase or reduction in interest rates) tends to change the EFP in the same direction. Thus the impact of monetary policy on the cost of borrowing is magnified because of the effect on the EFP.

Bernanke and Gertler (1995) describe two sub-channels of the credit channel: (1) the balance sheet channel (explains the potential impact of monetary policy on borrower's balance sheet and (2) the bank lending channel (focuses on the possible effects of monetary policy on the supply of loans by lenders). The latter is more important for the purpose of this study. Monetary policy affects the EFP by shifting the supply of intermediate credit, particularly loans by commercial banks. This is the bank-lending channel. Given the frictions in credit markets (e.g. an increase in information asymmetry or asymmetry of expectations), a reduction in the supply of bank loans for whatever reason may cause bank-dependent borrowers (e.g. SMEs) to have reduced access to credit and hence increase the external finance premium. They may not be totally constrained from obtaining credit, but they are virtually certain to incur costs associated with finding a new lender and establishing a credit relationship. The analysis of both the balance sheet and bank lending channels of the credit view also shows that the EFP increases for a longer time than the increase in short term interest rates, magnifying the effect of a policy-induced credit constraint.

6.1.4.2 The Credit Market Structure

The structure of the lending market banks operates in influences the profitability of commercial lending to SMEs. The bank market structure defines the degree of market concentration or competition among banks of similar or different characteristics, which in turn affects the level of profits they make. Recent evidence from Berger et al. (2007) show that market size structure[3] has been found to affect the quantity and price of loans to businesses by banks of different sizes. They found that large banks tend to charge lower premiums on loans than small banks and that this is so because large banks tend to operate in local markets with high market shares for large banks. Higher bank profits and interest margins would only be consistent with relatively weaker competition, supporting the notion of a negative relationship between competition and loan profitability (e.g. Short 1979). However, because of this inverse relationship between competition and loan profitability, banks now try to build comparative advantage, for example they offer relationship lending in order to diversify their services from those of other banks and, in the process, to earn more additional income. In addition, for post-Keynesians, competition is not determined solely by the number of players in the market but also by the rate of return that lenders expect from different borrowing groups (Basu 2003). So for example, there is more competition for large customers than small ones because they offer a higher expected rate of return.

6.1.4.3 Business Cycle Fluctuations

During a downward slope of the business cycle, the risk of business loans and the related capital requirements of banks tend to increase. There is therefore a danger that banks become less forthcoming in extending loans, thus reinforcing the cyclical slowdown in what is called a "credit crunch" (Bikker and Hu 2002). There is a possibility that loans will be extended less liberally during a cyclical downswing,

---

[3]Market size structure according to Berger et al. (2007) refers to the distribution of shares of different size classes of local market participants, where the sizes are inclusive of assets both within and outside the local market.

the argument being that risk premiums are, in fact, assumed to be insufficient cover for the increased risk or inadequate due to adverse selection and moral hazard problems (Stiglitz and Weiss 1981). Moreover, during a downswing, loan demand tends to be more interest elastic than during normal times.

6.2   Determinants of Collateral on SME Loans

As noted earlier, the theoretical literature on collateral demonstrates that collateral can be used to reduce adverse selection problems (Stiglitz and Weiss 1981; Chan and Kanatas 1985; Besanko and Thakor 1987a, b; Mishkin 2010). The following are the main drivers of the use and amount of collateralisation.

6.2.1   Collateral and Loan Characteristics

6.2.1.1   Loan Size

Generally, banks tend to request collateral from SMEs before making loans and banks' collateral requirement depends on the loan size, regardless of whether the firm is large or small. Jimenez et al. (2006) found a positive relationship between loan size and the probability of requesting collateral from SMEs and opined that loan size indicates a lender's relative increase in credit risk. However, predictions from Boot et al. (1991) and Jimenez et al. (2006) reveal that the amount of collateral pledged in a particular loan will increase if the loan is granted in a period of higher real interest rates and will decrease with the size of the loan. In many banks, collateral requirement usually amounts to 100 % (or more) of the loan size. The reason for banks requiring a high collateral-to-loan value reflects the lenders' consideration of the fact that small business borrowers will more likely default under poor economic circumstances when the value of their collateral is lower (Epstein and Graham 1991). Moreover, legal and practical problems of monitoring the collateral and gaining control of it at the time of default can be quite significant and costly.

6.2.1.2   Loan Purpose and Duration

Bank's collateral requirement also depends on the risk of loan default, which can be ascertained by the purpose of the loan and its duration. According to Cowling (1999), the purpose for which a loan is being requested is important in order to ascertain the riskiness of the loan contract. For example, the riskiness of a loan being used to finance investment in fixed assets will be different from the riskiness of a loan used as working capital or to finance cash expenses. To mitigate the risk of default associated with loan mismanagement or diversion and tie the incentives of the borrower with that of the lender, many banks request collateral. Long-term loans and short-term loans also explain the likelihood of collateral covering 100 % of the face value of the loan (full collateralisation) or the loan being only partially covered by the collateral (Jimenez et al. 2006).

6.2.2   Collateral and Borrower Risk Characteristics

6.2.2.1   Firm Size

Banks' collateral requirements are likely to differ between large and small firms. There is evidence to show that large prime borrowers are more likely to get unsecured funding because they tend to have stronger capital base, more diversified ownership structure, more stable cash flows and more certain investment opportunities. Berger and Udell (1990) and Cowling (1999), found a negative relationship between firm size and the incidence of loan collateralisation, since the probability of failure declines with size.

6.2.2.2   Firm Risk Rating

Banks' collateral requirement also depends on the firm's/owner's credit rating or number of delinquencies. If collateral is used as an incentive against borrower default, less credit worthy borrowers will be required to offer more collateral for a given size of loan (Boot et al. 1991; Chan and Kanatas 1985; Jimenez et al. 2006). According to Berger and Udell (1990), safer borrowers more often pledge collateral, which necessarily implies that secured loans are less risky than unsecured loans. Collateral can also be used as a signal of high credit quality in situations in which borrowers know their credit quality but lenders do not (Chan and Kanatas 1985; Besanko and Thakor 1987a). Besanko and Thakor (1987a) show that competition for loans results in every borrower being offered a contract that maximizes its expected utility subject to the constraint that the bank breaks even. They find that collateral plays a useful role. By designing credit contracts with inversely related interest rates and collateral requirements, banks can sort borrowers into risk classes. Low risk borrowers choose contracts with low interest rates and high collateral requirements whereas high-risk borrowers choose contracts with high interest rates and low collateral requirements. However, what happens in practice is somewhat different: large firm borrowers (which are low-risk compared to SMEs) are offered low interest rates (lower than SMEs) and collateral requirements are also lower.

6.2.3 Collateral and Lender Characteristics

Lender type, lender specialization and other differences in business model are likely to affect banks' decision on whether or not to request collateral from SMEs.

6.2.3.1 Collateralised Lending Versus Monitored Lending

The influence of lender characteristics on loan contracts determination can be explained by the approach to lending adopted, i.e. whether lending is secured or asset-backed (collateralised lending) or whether lending is information and relationship-driven (monitored lending). In collateralised lending, the borrower undertakes to relinquish ownership of a valuable asset to the lender if he or she fails to repay a loan. If the borrower defaults on the loan, the lender reserves the right to seize, sell or liquidate the asset and use the proceeds to offset the loan. Nakamura (1994) points out that 'because the lender has recourse to the collateral, the borrower has a strong incentive to repay the loan in full' (p. 8). However, it should be noted that that there are huge transaction costs involved with administering the sale of a collateralised property. Moreover, in some cases the value of the collateral may have diminished beyond the amount borrowed. Thus the gains to the lender might be modest (Cole et al. 2004).

In monitored lending, the lender closely monitors the financial condition of the borrower and intervenes quickly to protect its interest anytime it notices a sign that the borrower will default. The lender can threaten to refuse future loan requests or force bankruptcy (Nakamura 1994). Effective monitoring and gathering of additional information regarding the financial condition of the borrower will help the lender mitigate the risk of default (Diamond 1984). A major difference between collateralised lending and monitored lending is that in the former, the lender monitors the value of the collateral but is less concerned about the financial status of the borrower, whereas in monitored lending, the lender monitors the financial condition of the borrower and takes necessary actions when the risk of default is higher. Monitored lending therefore supports information disclosure and development of borrower-lender relationships.

6.2.3.2 Lender Type and Specialization

Jimenez et al. (2006) hypothesized that the use of collateral in loan contracting is a function of the type of lender. They emphasised that young and inexperienced banks with relatively lower expertise or specialization in loan contracting as well as fewer financial resources to assess the riskiness of borrowers are more likely to employ collateral as a substitute for such an evaluation. If this is the case, then it is expected that small banks will fall into this category and are likely to have incentive to demand collateral from applicants, especially those with low credit quality.

6.2.4   Collateral and Loan Relationships

As noted earlier, the length of borrower-lender relationships can influence the setting of loan contract terms. Boot and Thakor (1994) show that when lenders and borrowers engage in repeated interactions through time, they are able to build trust and credibility, which help to reduce moral hazard problems. Banks that have gathered proprietary information over their clients often use this information in refining contract terms offered to borrowers. Berger and Udell (1995) in their study of the role of relationships in determining both price and non-price contract terms of bank lines of credit extended to firms find that longer bank- borrower relationships reduce the interest rates paid by borrowers and the chances that they will have to pledge collateral. According to Boot et al. (1991), collateral is an alternative to trust and by developing relationships, it is expected that collateral requirements would be more relaxed. Jimenez et al. (2006) also found that the likelihood of collateral is lower for loans made to borrowers with longer relationship with the lender that grants the loan. To the extent that this occurs, longer duration of banking relationships relaxes the terms of a loan, ameliorates credit constraints and hence raises firm value.

6.2.5   Collateral and External Factors

Bank's collateral requirement also depends on external factors such as competition and the business cycle.

6.2.5.1   Competition

Besanko and Thakor (1987b) show that the competition facing firms lowers the rents of lenders and suggests that the use of collateral is more likely with competition than monopoly. Competition shortens the borrower-lender relationship and reduces the incentives to invest in the acquisition of soft information (Chan et al. 1986; Diamond 1991; Petersen and Rajan 1995). This could in turn increase asymmetric information and the riskiness of business loans. Accordingly, the likelihood of requesting collateral is higher with increased firm competition.

6.2.5.2   Macroeconomic Conditions

Not much is known about the effect of macroeconomic conditions such as the business cycle and monetary policy on the use of collateral. During economic downturns (i.e. reducing output growth), lenders are likely to request collateral. Similarly, in periods of tighter monetary policy or higher real interest rates, borrowers are less likely to use collateral than they are in periods of loose monetary policy (Jimenez et al. 2006). However, studies on the financial crises (e.g. Minsky 1986) suggest that when the economy is growing, lenders tend to relax their risk assessment criteria (and demand less collateral).

References

Athanasoglou PP, Brissimis SN, Delis MD (2008) Bank-specific, industry-specific and macroeconomic determinants of bank profitability. Int Financ Markets Inst Money 18:121–136

Basu S (2003) Why do banks fail? Int Rev Appl Econ 17(3):231–248

Behr P, Guttler A (2007) Credit risk assessment and relationship lending: an empirical analysis of German small and medium-sized enterprises. J Small Bus Manage 45(2):194–213

Berger AN, Udell GF (1990) Collateral, loan quality and bank risk. J Monetary Econ 25:21–42

Berger AN, Udell GF (1995) Relationship lending and lines of credit in small firm finance. J Bus 68:351–382

Berger AN, Udell GF (2006) A more complete conceptual framework for financing of small and medium enterprises. J Finance Bank 30(11):2945–2966

Berger AN, Rosen RJ, Udell GF (2007) Does market size structure affect competition? The case of small business lending. J Bank Finance 31:11–33 (Elsevier)

Berger AN, Frame WS, Ioannidou V (2011) Reexamining the empirical relation between loan risk and collateral: the roles of collateral characteristics and types. Federal Reserve Bank of Atlanta Working Paper Series 2011–12

Berlin M, Mester L (1998) On the profitability and cost of relationship lending. J Bank Finance 22:873–897

Bernanke BS, Gertler M (1995) Inside the black box: the credit channel of monetary policy transmission. J Econ Perspect 9(4):27–48

Besanko D, Thakor AV (1987a) Collateral and rationing: sorting equilibria in monopolistic and competitive markets. Int Econ Rev 28:671–689

Besanko D, Thakor AV (1987b) Competitive equilibria in the credit market under asymmetric information. J Econ Theor 42:167–182

Bikker JA, Hu H (2002) Cyclical patterns in profits, provisioning and lending of banks. DNB Staff Reports No. 86 De Nederlandsche Bank NV

Boot AWA (2000) Relationship banking: what do we know? J Financ Intermediation 9:7–25

Boot AWA, Thakor AV (1994) Moral hazard and secured lending in an infinitely repeated credit market game. Int Econ Rev 35:899–920

Boot AWA, Thakor AV, Udell GF (1991) Secured lending and default risk: equilibrium analysis, policy implications and empirical results. Econ J 101:458–472

Bruns V, Fletcher M (2008) Banks' risk assessment of Swedish SMEs. Venture Capital 10 (2):171–194

Chan YS, Kanatas G (1985) Asymmetric valuation and the role of collateral in loan agreements. J Money Credit Bank 17(1):85–95

Chan YS, Greenbaum SI, Thakor AV (1986) Information reusability, competition and bank asset quality. J Bank Finance 10:255–276

Churchill NC, Lewis VL (1986) Bank lending to new and growing enterprises. J Bus Ventur 1:193–206

Cole RA, Goldberg LG, White LJ (2004) Cookie-cutter versus character: the micro structure of small business lending by large and small banks. J Financ Quant Anal 39(2):227–251

Cowling M (1999) The incidence of loan collateralisation in small business lending contracts: evidence from the UK. Appl Econ Lett 6(5):291–293

D'Auria C, Foglia A, Reedtz PM (1999) Bank interest rates and credit relationships in Italy. J Bank Finance 23:1067–1093

Diamond DW (1984) Financial intermediation and delegated monitoring. Rev Econ Stud 51:393–414

Diamond DW (1989) Reputation acquisition in debt markets. J Polit Econ 97(4):828–862

Diamond DW (1991) Monitoring and reputation: the choice between bank loans and directly placed debt. J Polit Econ 99:689–721

Diamond DW, Dybvig P (1983) Bank runs, deposit insurance and liquidity. J Polit Econ 91:401–419

Epstein J, Graham F (1991) The role of collateral in small business lending. Research Paper prepared for the office of investment, Bureau for Private Enterprises, U.S. Agency for International Development (USAID), PN-ABN-271

Brunnermeier M, Crockett A, Goodhart,CA, Persaud A, Shin HS (2009) The fundamental principles of financial regulation. Geneva Reports on the World Economy. International Centre for Monetary and Banking Studies, London

Gup BE, Walter JR (1989) Top performing small banks: making money the old-fashioned way. Fed Reserve Bank Richmond Econ Rev 75:23–35

Harhoff D, Korting T (1998) Lending relationships in Germany: empirical results from survey data. J Bank Finance 22:1317–1354

Haynes GW, Ou C, Berney R (1999) Small business borrowing from large and small banks. In: Blanton JL, Williams A, Rhine SLW Business Access to Capital and Credit. A federal reserve system research conference, pp 287–327

Hubbard G, Kuttner K, Palia D (2002) Are there bank effects in borrowers' costs of funds? Evidence from a matched sample of borrowers and banks. J Bus 75(4):559–581

Hyytinen A, Pajarinen M (2008) Opacity of young businesses: evidence from rating disagreements. J Bank Finance 32:1234–1241

Jimenez G, Saurina J (2004) Collateral, type of lender and relationship banking as determinants of credit risk. J Bank Finance 28:2191–2212

Jimenez G, Salas V, Saurina J (2006) Determinants of collateral. J Financ Econ 81:255–281

Lefilleur J (2009) Financing SMEs in a context of strong information asymmetry. Private Sect Dev 1:13–15

Lehmann E, Neuberger D (2001) Do lending relationships matter? Evidence from bank survey data in Germany. J Econ Behav Organ 45:339–359

Machauer A, Weber M (1998) Bank behaviour based on internal credit ratings of borrowers. J Bank Finance 22:1355–1383

Minsky H (1986) Stabilizing an unstable economy. Yale University Press, New Haven

Mishkin FS (2010) The economics of money, banking and financial markets, 9th edn. Pearson, London, p 664

Nakamura LI (1994) Small borrowers and the survival of the small bank: is mouse bank mighty or Mickey? Federal Reserve Bank of Philadelphia Business Review, pp 3–15

Petersen MA, Rajan RG (1994) The benefits of firm-creditor relationships: evidence from small business data. J Finance 49:3–37

Petersen MA, Rajan RG (1995) The effect of credit market competition on lending relationship. Q J Econ 110:407–443

Rajan RG (1992) Insiders and outsiders: the choice between informed and arm's-length debt. J Finance 47:1367–1400

Sharpe SA (1990) Asymmetric information, bank lending, and implicit contracts: a stylized model of customer relationships. J Finance 45:1069–1087

Short BK (1979) The relation between commercial bank profit rates and banking concentration in Canada, Western Europe, and Japan. J Bank Finance 3:209–219

Stiglitz J, Weiss A (1981) Credit rationing in markets with imperfect information. Am Econ Rev
71:393–410

St-Pierre J, Bahri M (2011) The determinants of risk premium: the case of bank lines of credit
granted to SMEs. J Dev Entrepreneurship 16(4):459–476

Wolfson MH (1996) A post Keynesian theory of credit rationing. J Post Keynesian Econ 18
(3):443–470

Chapter 7
Conclusions and Practical Implications

This study has examined a great deal of theoretical and empirical literature on the demand and supply side factors affecting bank involvement with SMEs. It has been established that access to bank finance for SMEs is difficult and costly because they are relatively young and informationally opaque. SMEs tend to rely much on bank finance not just for their operational needs but also in order to build credit reputation early in their life cycle. The theoretical models upon which the foundation of bank lending is carried out are the money creation and credit rationing concepts. The literature revealed a number of debates on the relative role of money demand and supply in determining lending constraints. The post-Keynesians explain that banks do not simply act as intermediaries, lending out savings deposits, but tend to create deposits by extending loans, a phenomenon that is contrary to the so-called money multiplier theory. Mainstream economic theory assumes that asymmetric information is widespread in financial markets and that with the presence of "adverse selection" and "moral hazard" effects, credit rationing may persist even in liberalised financial markets. For post-Keynesians, information asymmetry is unrealistic because fundamental uncertainty exists in an investment project, so that both the lender and borrower are oblivious of the riskiness of the project. For post-Keynesians, the main constraints to bank lending are the changes in the financial condition of borrowers (e.g. amount of indebtedness, cash flow, liquidity and financial fragility, etc.), which implies that banks also change their valuation of the riskiness of the borrowers. To mitigate information asymmetry problems, bankers may adopt a number of precautionary measures, such as requiring that financing be collateralized or guaranteed, adopting restrictive loan covenants and entering into fee-based loan commitments over the life of a bank-borrower relationship. If the bank's terms are not met, they may simply turn down the request for financing ('credit rationing').

The factors affecting the supply of credit to SMEs can be categorized into demand-side and supply-side factors. In particular, on the demand-side, borrower characteristics such as firm and owner characteristics, and the nature of borrower-lender relationships affect the underwriting practices of banks. Findings generally reveal that a borrower's size, credit reputation, availability and cost of proprietary information and bank size play a major role in a borrower's choice of financing source. Large banks tend to be attracted to larger, older, well established

© The Author(s) 2016
V.U. Ekpu, *Determinants of Bank Involvement with SMEs*,
SpringerBriefs in Finance, DOI 10.1007/978-3-319-25837-9_7

and more financially secure firms, while smaller (relationship-driven) banks tend to pay more attention to applicants that have pre-existing loan and deposit relationships with them. Banks are also more likely to demand collateral from young and inexperienced SME borrowers. This is because SMEs are known to be risky and have high failure rate. While smaller banks have longer and more exclusive personal relationships with SME borrowers, large multi-office banks tend to have more short-lived, less exclusive and distant relationships with their customers. Empirical evidence reveals that longer firm-borrower relationships help to reduce loan prices and collateral requirements of firms, thereby increasing firm value.

On the supply side, bank organizational structure, regulatory requirements, the type of lending technology adopted, and the bank market structure are dominant factors. Banks that have a relatively flatter organizational structure (such as smaller banks) tend to have advantages in loan monitoring and increased loan officer discretion. However, large banks with multi-office structures find it extremely costly to invest in relationships. Banks that are largely geared towards SMEs are known to be heavily reliant on relationship lending techniques, while large multi-office banks tend to have advantages in economies of scale and scope because they rely on transactions-based lending and other financial management services. Regulatory factors such as enforcement of capital requirements, sectoral credit limits and monetary policies also affect the quantity and cost of loanable funds via lenders' risk appetite, credit rationing and the credit channel, respectively. Banking consolidation also tends to affect SME lending. Empirical findings reveal that a large bank acquisition of a small bank often reduces SME lending in the short run, but this effect is offset in the long run by the decision of other small banks to increase lending to SMEs. Lastly, commercial lending is also affected by the structure of the banking market. This manifests in two forms: *product* and *geographic* market competition. Smaller banks tend to specialize in SME loans because they are unable to compete with larger banks for larger loans in order to keep up with regulatory limits on loan concentration. Moreover, they cannot offer a wide range of financial services, as do larger banks. Local and regional banks tend to situate their offices mostly in (less competitive) rural areas, while large banks operate in urban areas where most large businesses are found. However, with changes in regulation, large banks now penetrate rural banking markets, raising questions regarding the survivability of small local banks and bank-dependent small business borrowers located in those regions.

Technological innovations have transformed the financial services industry from a local to a global market. With revolutions in technology, many banks, especially large ones now rely significantly on credit scoring to assess the riskiness of less transparent small business borrowers. This automated lending process makes it easier for large banks to make large pool of loans faster, cheaper and over great distances. While this is a good development in itself, there are particularly important implications for smaller banks that tend to rely hugely on relationship loans for their profitability and survival. Most researchers believe that credit scoring as a lending technology is mostly associated with large banks because they are able to build more reliable proprietary models from a large pool of loan database. The implication of this is that while large banks enjoy potential economies of scale from dealing with high-volume loan applications, smaller banks do not have sufficient loan volume to develop their own proprietary models. Thus smaller banks still tend to utilize relationship lending because they believe that relationship provides them with a competitive advantage. This study, however, demonstrates that both large and small banks can potentially benefit from credit scoring though with some downsides. However, by investing more in small business credit scoring, small banks can complement the personalized services they render to local customers and thus mitigate their cost disadvantages with respect to large banks. In addition to the use of relationship lending and credit scoring techniques, banks, particularly in developing credit markets are increasingly embracing other cutting edge techniques in assessing borrowers, such as psychometric scoring and judgmental score cards. Technological revolutions in advanced credit markets have also made electronic marketplaces possible, such as in peer-to-peer lending, where borrowers place request for loans online and private lenders bid to fund these loans.

This study also considered the determination of loan contracts on SME loans. The determinants of risk premium on SME loans are largely connected with factors that underline the opacity and riskiness of SMEs such as firm size, firm age, firm credit rating, and availability of collateral. Risk premium is also affected by bank-borrower relationship factors as well as the lender's cost of funds and administrative expenses associated with loan appraisal and disbursement. The determinants of use and amount of collateral are largely associated with borrower and loan characteristics, particularly firm size, loan size and borrower's credit rating. External factors such as the business cycle, competition and other market structure factors also affect the extent to which collateral is used to secure credit transactions.

Overall, this study has provided useful insights into the influence of demand side factors, bank-level factors and other external factors on SME lending practices. The findings from this study will be of interest to stakeholders in the SME lending market, particularly government and economic policy makers, bankers and bank-dependent small business borrowers. Economic policy makers can understand from this study the factors affecting lenders' decisions to lend to SMEs including the factors that affect the quantity and cost of credit available to SMEs, which is crucial for improving SME lending policies. The firm-specific, bank-specific and external constraints often cited as affecting the profitability of SME loans reinforce the role of the government in providing an enabling environment for encouraging competition and innovation in SME lending. This survey also helps to provide direction for government in the area of improving the lending infrastructure— namely improving the economics of information, improving the legal, judicial and bankruptcy environment and improving the tax and regulatory environments. These will, in turn, help to reduce the cost of doing business and promote competition and profitability of bank loans.

Banks may especially benefit from this study as it might help them to understand the profitability and economics of their lending methods, policies, and business models and how to improve their SME risk management practices. Specifically, they may understand the economic value or benefits of relationship lending to their bank and how to strengthen their relationship-banking model and develop new and innovative techniques for lending to SMEs at this time where increasing bank competition, technological advancements and alternative financing sources are changing the trends in SME banking.

Finally, It is intended that the findings of this survey will also help improve the knowledge of bank-dependent SME borrowers with respect to understanding banks' requirements and expectations for loan applicants and users of loanable funds in order to better satisfy their banking and financial needs. The opacity and riskiness of SMEs as revealed by this study further reinforce the role of education and training for entrepreneurs/borrowers on business and financial management skills.

15586330R00061

Printed in Great Britain
by Amazon